BASS LURES

Tricks & Techniques

New, Innovative Ways To Fish Artificial Baits

by Larry Larsen

Book IV in the Bass Series Library

A LARSEN'S OUTDOOR PUBLISHING BOOK
THE ROWMAN & LITTLEFIELD PUBLISHING GROUP, INC.
Lanham • Chicago • New York • Toronto • Plymouth, UK

Published by
LARSEN'S OUTDOOR PUBLISHING
An imprint of The Rowman & Littlefield Publishing Group, Inc.
4501 Forbes Boulevard, Suite 200, Lanham, Maryland 20706
http://www.rlpgtrade.com

Estover Road, Plymouth PL6 7PY, United Kingdom

Distributed by National Book Network

British Library Cataloguing in Publication Information Available

Library of Congress Cataloging-in-Publication Data Available

Library of Congress 87-82758

ISBN: 978-0-936513-02-7 (paper : alk.paper)

♾™ The paper used in this publication meets the minimum
requirements of American National Standard for Information
Sciences—Permanence of Paper for Printed Library Materials,
ANSI/NISO Z39.48-1992.

Printed in the United States of America

DEDICATION

To my wife Lilliam, for supporting my happiness and my life and career objectives.

ACKNOWLEDGMENTS

The valuable assistance of the many magazine editors and publishers, and outdoor book reviewers who helped to make my previous books a success, is much appreciated. Such motivation will continue to generate a desire to create additional reading for America's bass anglers. Thanks go to all the industry lure manufacturers, without whom we wouldn't have such productive choices available today.

I wish to also thank those guides and professional anglers with whom, for the past 25 years, I have shared a boat, their friendship and experiences. Rick Clunn, Larry Nixon, Ken Cook, Tommy Martin, Ron Shearer, Randy Fite, Harold Allen, Randy Dearman, Jack Westberry, Larry Lazoen, Wayne Yohn, Lee Sisson and Dr. Loren Hill all deserve my gratitude for their contribution to the sport.

Just as importantly, my appreciation also goes to the interested bass fishermen everywhere that seek more knowledge about their favorite pastime. That keeps me going.

PREFACE

Lures have been fooling largemouth bass for years, and they always will. They are ever-changing though; they need to be, in order to be successful.

Modifications of lures and development of new baits and techniques continue to keep the fare fresh, and that's important. Bass seem to become "accustomed" to the same artificials and presentations seen over and over again. As a result, they become harder to catch. It's the new approach that again sparks the interest of some largemouth.

To that end, this book explores some of the latest ideas for modifying, rigging and using bass lures. All are highly productive when utilized in the correct environment and conditions. Many lure modifications and techniques presented within these covers are unique, and angler success with them has tended to motivate additional lure development.

The tricks and techniques outlined in this book should work anywhere in the country. Some were generated in the far West, others have been successful in a tiny locale for years, but the word is spreading fast. Still other productive concepts revealed in this book were developed on highly-vegetated southeast waters. "BASS LURES—Tricks & Techniques" will help anglers everywhere to catch more fish.

CONTENTS

ABOUT THE AUTHOR

Writing about bass fishing for more than 16 years, Larry Larsen has studied all aspects of the fish, and the ways to catch them. He has previously published three books "Follow The Forage For Better Bass Angling," "Shallow Water Bass," and "Bass Pro Strategies."

Larsen's writings detail highly productive fish catching methods and special techniques. He believes in explaining to readers the latest and very best tactics to find and catch bass anywhere. The basis of utilizing lures with innovative modifications and techniques to catch more and larger bass is presented in this book as an extension of that philosophy.

The author has been a frequent contributor on bass subjects to *Outdoor Life, Sports Afield, Fishing Facts,* and *Field & Stream.* More than 700 of Larsen's magazine articles have been published in 50 different publications, including credits in *Bassin', Bassmaster, Bass Illustrated, U.S. Bass, Petersen's Fishing,* and other major outdoor magazines.

Larry Larsen's photography has appeared on the covers of many national publications. Larsen is a member of the Outdoor Writers Association of America (OWAA), the Southeastern Outdoor Press Association (SEOPA), and the Florida Outdoor Writers Association (FOWA). Larsen has been honored with several regional and national awards over the years for both outdoor writing and photography.

The first chapter in this book is similar in part to an article that won him second place in the 1986 OWAA Crankbait Techniques Writing Contest. Another of Larsen's how-to articles on lure techniques captured first place in that same category in the 1987 contest, a feat he'll long remember. The magazine article competition is the most popular contest among OWAA's professional outdoor writers and included over 1,000 entries each year.

Larry Larsen, who is a graduate of Wichita State University and Colorado State University, is an accomplished fisherman as well as a

successful outdoor writer/photographer. His angling adventures and research on the black bass have been extensive throughout the southern and midwestern states. He has caught and released numerous big bass, over 100 between five and 12 pounds, on artificial lures.

Larsen has literally traveled the globe to fish for bass. He has jigged for bass from lakes near the Canadian border and tossed giant worms into Honduras' Lake Yojoa, some 3,500 miles to the south. He has pursued bass with top water buzz baits as far east as Cuba's Treasure Lake and taken largemouth on crankbaits from plantation lakes in the Hawaiian Islands some 6,000 miles to the west.

Anglers that apply the information contained within these covers will greatly benefit. The book details productive tricks and tactics that any angler, novice or professional, can apply to catch more bass on artificial lures. Numerous photographs and figures help detail productive lure methods to entice America's most popular game fish.

INTRODUCTION

TODAY'S TACKLE BOX

State Of The Art Bass Fishing Lures

THEY RATTLE, FLASH, give off an attractant scent and come in every color in the rainbow. They supposedly even taste like something alive. They are made of space-age materials and some even sport "stealth hardware." They are the state-of-the-art in bass lures. The assortment of new and unique fare being offered to America's most popular sport fish is dazzling.

Lure makers have always put major emphasis on the looks and action of their artificial baits. Obviously, a cosmetically-attractive plug will sell better to the angler; to that end, the photo-print and detailed paint finishes and hand-sculpted lines applied to many lures in the past few years is unsurpassed.

Realism in the form of forage color and shape imitation has been refined to an art. Shelves in tackle shops are stocked with "natural" frogs, snakes, eels, shad, shiners, bluegil and crayfish. Just how some of the artificial creations can "live out of the water" can amaze some.

The trends in recent years have been toward bass lures that have more appeal to the fish senses. Bass use their sense of sight, hearing, smell and taste to find and eat forage. Fisheries biologists have conducted valuable research in the past several years on bass' ability to distinguish between certain colors, to hear certain sounds and detect specific attracting or alarming smells.

The forage preferences of bass based on their interpretation of sensual feedback is better defined now, allowing lure manufacturers to apply that knowledge. And, that they have.

Selection Of Colors

The latest trend in coloration of bass lures is based upon years of research performed by Dr. Loren Hill, Department Head of Zoology at the University of Oklahoma. He discovered that bass see colors in all water conditions, and which of those colors would be more likely to trigger aggressive responses.

In the spring of 1985, Lake Systems Division of Mt. Vernon, Missouri, introduced the Color-C-Lector, a battery-powered instrument based on Dr. Hill's extensive testing. On the face of the new "tool" was a color spectrum of 20 basic and six fluorescent colors, specifically laid out on three water-clarity scales. By lowering a probe over the boat's side, anglers were able to determine the optimal lure color to fish.

Few technological advances in the history of bass fishing lures have had the impact of the Color-C-Lector. The instrument immediately captured the interest of fishermen and lure makers. Tackle shelves took on a new look with a dazzling variety of colors: fluorescent orange, pinks, lime, purple, wine, peach, etc. So did tackle boxes, and anglers were soon catching lots of bass on old lures sporting the new color schemes.

Another lure coloration innovation in plugs is toward reflective prismatic colors. Several baits with prism inserts reflect the colors around them. Many lure manufacturers now offer prismatic crankbaits that scatter different colors. Some use special reflective coatings to enhance the "flash appeal."

Hard-Body And Soft Plastic Fare

The very latest trend in diving plugs is the deep runners, those that approach or exceed 20 feet. Most crankbait manufacturers have a "20-footer" in their line. While some of the older plugs ran close to that depth, the marketing of depth is now the focus. These new lipped baits dive to attract bass never before reached.

Shot-filled cavities that emit a rattling sound as the plug vibrates through the water are as popular with bass as ever. Most hard-bodied lure manufacturers at least offer the rattle option in their line. The fact that even muddy-water bass can detect the sound vibration of a live or artificial bait moving several feet away makes that an important consideration.

The "smell craze" is upon us as more and more "attractant" products are offered in both liquid and solid form. Attention to the bass sense of smell has finally blossomed. Some lure manufacturers have built in a "pocket" or holding means for the application of an attractor. Other lures are coated with an adherent surface coating in which a spray-on formula can be utilized.

Worms of soft plastic that incorporate unique design features and salt or other bass attractants are most productive today.

Obviously, the hard-bodied baits have more problems in offering either a built-in attractant or the carrying capability. Plastic worms, snakes and eels often have a "secret smell agent" in the formula prior to being injection molded. Many in the past few years have had their taste enhanced. The addition of salt to the soft plastics seems to increase fishing success.

The trend in plastics has always been to give the baits a self-induced action that attracts the bass. To that end, manufacturers have added curly tails, warts, rings, multiple wings and tails and hollow bodies. Special flippin' baits designed especially to work in dense cover and attract bass are now found in tackle boxes. These lures are usually thick bodied, large-silhouette snake imitations with a huge curl tail that provide maximum action.

More Innovations

New skirt colors and materials have been introduced on spinner-baits and jigs. Buzz baits, those that whip up the surface with a multi-blade prop, have been around for a few years but are growing in popularity. More weedless surface spinners are available now than ever before, and they often slay the bass.

Lure designs specifically for after-dark fishing have increased, and several manufacturers now offer artificials that glow in the dark. Spinnerbaits, jigs, crankbaits and worms with phosphorous paints and lighted inserts now "wake up" bass under the moonlight.

Techniques and modifications are on-going in this sport. There is always a new way to rig or alter an existing lure, and all the different ways to effectively fish even what is already in production have yet to be discovered. Professional tournament anglers, guide and resourceful weekend anglers are still coming up with new, productive ways to fish artificial baits.

Add to that the fact that much of the lure technology of today is based on scientific research not available five years ago, and the angler has more reason than ever to get out on the water. It all translates to better lures and still plenty of bass encounters.

Spinnerbaits that probe shallow, dense vegetation come in a variety of exciting skirt colors which bass are able to see better, under certain conditions.

Although bass are not as numerous, today's lures are more effective than those from yesteryear. With the fishing pressure that most waters receive, bass have become "wiser" in order to survive. Until anglers become accustomed to fishing bass for sport and releasing a majority of what they catch, the reality is that artificials will continuously need to evolve into even better lures to catch the fewer bass that remain.

The techniques and modifications or tricks presented in this book are not meant to be inclusive. They could never be. They are, however, highly productive ways to increase an angler's catch. If reading about some of the innovative methods and riggings moves an angler to think of an new idea that he wishes to try, then great. If the idea works, I hope that he'll let me in on the secret!

CHAPTER 1

CRANKBAITING TECHNIQUES

Proven Theories And Concepts

THE KEY TO PRODUCTIVE crankbait fishing is to keep the plug hitting something. The speed at which you are reeling it, or the size of the lure, is not as important. It must be bouncing off logs, weeds, or the bottom a great deal of the time, according to Montgomery, Texas, bass guide and touring pro, Rick Clunn.

He is a long-time practitioner of the diving plugs and a master at fishing them. He has developed specific criteria upon which to base his crankbait selection and technique. Clunn credits the bait with his first Classic win in 1976 and "making his whole career." He has done a lot with crankbaits since then.

"Crankbaits always play a role in my fishing," he says. "You don't always end up catching all your fish on them in a tournament, but you can learn so much about the water when you practice with them. You may find hidden structure below the surface and then switch to a different lure to more effectively fish a spot."

Successful fishing rests on your ability to use time wisely. The crankbait not only catches bass while you're covering a lot of water, but it helps you learn that water. Clunn firmly believes the bait allows an angler to find bass habitat that people throwing other lures won't discover.

People often don't get excited about fishing crankbaits until they see a catch of 75 pounds, then they get excited. A crankbait will make you work for fish, but with it you can cover a lot of water in a day's time. Most people have a limited amount of time to find fish, and no bait can cover water any faster than a crankbait!

"It is not a fun bait," admits Clunn. "You can't go out there and expect vicious strikes, although occasionally one will almost knock the rod out of your hands. You also may catch doubles on it and there's not many other type lures that will."

19

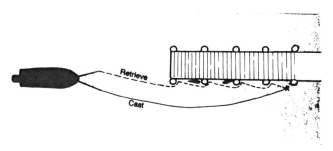

FIGURE 1—*A crankbait can be 'tuned' to run left or right by slightly bending the tie-eye in the opposite direction that you want the lure to run. The shady side of a dock or other obstruction can be more effectively fished with such a bait. Strikes will usually occur after the crankbait ricochets off a support post.*

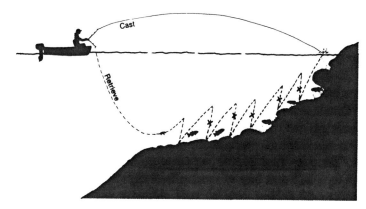

FIGURE 2—*The stop-and-go technique is a deadly method to attract largemouth bass. The retrieve pause will inspire 'lazy' predators to feed. Most strikes will occur as the plug floats back up from its point of contact with the bottom.*

Material Maneuvers

There are two basic types of crankbaits: wood baits and plastic baits. Selecting which to use is normally based on certain conditions.

Plastic baits are usually associated with slightly colder water, mainly because fish metabolism is slower and the best retrieve is a slower presentation. Bass in cold waters relate more to the bottom and tend to be less aggressive, so plastic baits could be productive.

When the water temperature drops to about 60 degrees, start thinking about slowing the bait down. In warmer temperatures, you can get away with a faster retrieve.

An additional advantage of fishing plastic baits slowly is that they don't have the buoyancy of wood working against them. You can crank them down deep, and then slow them down.

"When you slow down wood baits, they'll try to come back up off the bottom," Clunn points out. "Plastic baits also tend to have a wider wobble, and in cold water I like my bait to wobble wider from side to side at slow speeds. Most wooden baits, however, have much less vibration."

Plastic baits are ideal for fishing at night or in off-color water because the lure's side to side wobble displaces more water. Bass under those conditions seldom rely on their sight but depend more on their built-in "sonar system," the lateral line to find what they will eat. Clunn, who tosses a crankbait over 200 days each year, feels that plastic baits that displace more water are a little easier for the bass to find.

"I like to use the wooden baits in the warm-weather months when I'm fishing fairly fast," says Clunn. "In clearer waters, I tend

Crankbaits are adorned with more color today, thanks to fishery research into the senses of fish.

21

to really 'burn' a crankbait. When I am reeling the bait that fast, I prefer the wood versions because they have very fine vibration. They move more like shad."

Body And Bill Benefits

The crankbait is probably the most versatile tool of all lures. Due to the different bills and sizes, you can work depths efficiently from one foot down to about 22. It can be used in almost any body of water and in a variety of bass habitats.

Selection of crankbait size should be based upon several things, the most obvious being the available food supply at that time of year. If there are lots of small fry around in the late spring and early summer, then use smaller crankbaits. In the fall and winter, when everything has matured, go to larger baits.

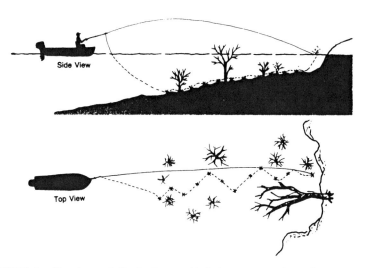

FIGURE 3—*'Burning and digging' a crankbait is an extremely productive way to trigger strikes. The lure is reeled as fast as possible, continuously making contact with the bottom. This causes a 'puff' of dirt or sand at each spot encountered. The high-speed retrieve will also cause the lure to wander erratically, often changing directions.*

Naturally, if there is a 15-inch length limit on the waters you're fishing, you'll probably throw a big bait most of the time. So if you're trying to catch bigger fish—and I believe in the old adage that 'big baits catch bigger fish—then fish a bigger bait. If, on the other hand, you are just trying to get a limit, go to smaller crankbaits that will attract bass of all sizes.

Lure size selection may also be determined by the color of the water. In murky or off-color water, fatter plastic baits that displace more water may be the better choice. In extremely clear water, a fast-moving bait with more natural colors would usually be more productive.

The bill shape and length is often more critical than the body size. The bill controls the depth of the lure and its size usually determines whether or not you are getting down deep enough to ricochet off the available cover.

"If I'm trying to fish a 45-degree angle bank with stumps and rocks on it, then I would use a deep diving bait," states Clunn. "I'll cast it to the shallows and dig it until the lure moves on down and stays on the bottom for a long time. If I'm fishing heavy, shallow cover, say two to three feet, I don't need a deep diving bait," he points out. "I can get deep enough bouncing a shallow runner through the stuff and seldom get hung up."

"The crankbait is just a tool," states Clunn, "and you have to learn the appropriate size of bill needed for the tool to cover the depth of water that you want to fish."

Fishing And Flexing Factors

The rod is also extremely critical in crankbait fishing, according to the three-time BASS Master Classic champion.

"Many people won't throw crankbaits for long because they are too tiring," says Clunn. "I used to fish them on a conventional 5 1/2-foot rod and they wore me out. I was trying to fight that bait all day long with just my wrist."

"The crankbait is a fast-moving bait, and I feel that they should be fished with a glass or glass-tip type rod," he says. "A fish will move on the fast-moving bait and try to inhale it and something has got to give it to him. A glass rod allows the fish to get it a little better than the high reflex-recovery, high-tech rods."

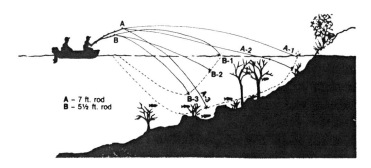

FIGURE 4—*The advantages of a seven-foot rod (A) versus that of a 5 1/2 footer (B) are further casting distance and a deeper lure trajectory (providing more time in the productive strike zone). The crankbait on the two rods are shown at lure touchdown (1), after four turns of the reel handle (2), and half-way into the retrieve (3).*

"You don't have to determine strikes on a crankbait. That's the key to the productivity of the glass rods," he explains. "The high-tech rods work to your disadvantage there too. Not only do they have fast flex recovery, but you're working a fast bait and you react faster when you feel the strike," he says. "All of that goes into hooking the fish very poorly, whereas when a crankbait is moving fast and you have your hooks right, the fish will hook itself."

"Only on a worm-type bait do you want to feel the fish inhaling the bait," Clunn says. "With a crankbait, I want to be behind the fish. I want the rod to flex and give the bait to him, and I don't even want to set the hook until he's closed on the bait. The response feels more sluggish and that's contrary to what our modern minds have learned is right."

Distance And Depth Dependence

"The smartest thing that I ever did was go to a long handle, 7-foot rod that I can brace against my wrist and against my side," he says. "When throwing the crankbait, I can use two hands and really

24

put the bait out there a long way. With most bass fishing, distance is not necessary, but I think long casts are usually necessary when fishing crankbaits."

Clunn explains, "That bait comes back in a parabolic-type curve and it reaches its maximum depth at the bottom. Then the bait starts coming back up at the boat. The longer that you can keep it at that maximum depth, the more contact your bait will usually make, and consequently you'll catch more fish."

On a short cast, that bait won't stay down as long, so the bait's coverage at maximum depth is minimal. The long cast is very beneficial in crankbait fishing and the long rod, correspondingly, helps you to cast the lure further.

How you hold the rod also influences how deep the bait runs. If you put the rod tip down below the surface of the water, the bait will

The silver or white-sided baits, often with black backs, resemble the popular bass forage, threadfin shad. They continue to outproduce most colors.

achieve a deeper depth. Most cranking experts will normally try to cast their lures as far as they can, about 40 yards usually, and retrieve with the tip down.

The line also can control the depth of the lure. Clunn doesn't often vary the line size. Although occasionally he'll go to heavier line, he normally fishes 15-pound test. Rather than drop down in line size to get a bait to run deeper, he will use a different bill to achieve that; that's the value of knowing the depths at which your baits will run on a certain pound test.

The only reason to drop to a lighter pound test line is for use in clear water, when you really want to get the bait to maximum depth. The crankbait is normally digging into underwater structures, and with 10-pound monofilament, you're going to lose a lot more baits or waste a lot more time going after them. With heavier line you have a better chance of pulling them loose.

"A crankbait is one of the least fished baits," says Clunn, "and it's not an exciting one either. I wouldn't even qualify it as fun compared to other baits." he says. "Few fishermen really want to throw them, but it's still a very good bait!"

"Fish relate to angling pressure. If everyone is throwing a spinnerbait along a weedline, I may go to a small crankbait, even though it might be spinnerbait-type water," explains Clunn. "Changing the lure that the fish sees may make a big difference."

Cast And Crank Variations

Bass may not see as many crankbaits, nor do they see many baits at typical crankbait depths. Most anglers will fish a worm right on the bottom, or will fish a plug or spinnerbait near the surface. Those areas receive the most pressure, and the in between zones are pretty much neglected.

Most of the strikes will come when the bait is hitting something, and that usually occurs at the deepest contact point more than any other time. The second most common place to get a strike is right at the boat, as the bait comes off the bottom and heads to the surface. Anglers should also be very conscious of what they're doing with the

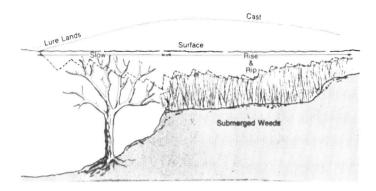

FIGURE 5—*The key to a lure attracting strikes is being in contact with something most times. Slow a retrieve to allow the lure to go up and down all branches on a submerged tree. When fishing hydrilla or submerged vegetation with crankbaits, you can effectively 'rip' the lure into and through the soft upper shoots of plants. If the aquatic weeds are tough, then use the rip-and-pause method. You have to penetrate such cover to trigger the strikes.*

trolling motor when the bait is nearing the boat. It is very important at that point to expect a strike.

"Our trolling motors are getting more and more powerful and we tend to emphasize move, move, move," Clunn says. "The minute that my bait approaches the boat, I get off the motor switch and give the fish an opportunity to hit."

Clunn rarely varies the retrieve. Most of the time he'll let the objects vary the retrieve. Occasionally he will consciously stop the lure, especially when fishing during the colder months, or if casting to a key spot where he has pinpointed bass.

"I depend mostly on deflection of the bait for strikes and that comes from hitting stuff," says Clunn. "The second best technique for me is the stop-and-go retrieve. I'll just reel it very fast, stop, and hold it."

"Normally I'll find out they want this presentation when my bait is stopped by a limb and doesn't deflect over it. One or two strikes in this instance should tell me something," he says. "I'll then intentionally use the stop-and-go retrieve each time the bait ticks something. That's just being observant and paying attention to what the fish is trying to tell you."

CHAPTER 2

CRANKBAIT CAPABILITIES

Design Variations For Productivity

GOOD CRANKBAIT FISHERMEN are going to lose a number of baits and they can't be afraid of losing them. The angler needs to run the bait into logs and brush to get the majority of non aggressive bass. If he gets the bait to deflect off the structure, he has doubled his chance of getting a fish.

In order to keep the bait in contact with either the structure or the bottom, you have to get it to descend to the appropriate depth. That is a problem for some anglers, according to most lure designers. They, more than any others, are aware of what many fishermen do (or don't do) with those baits.

"A lot of people think that the harder you crank a diving plug, the deeper it'll go," says lure designer Lee Sisson. "The truth is that you can actually over-crank it, and it's not only unloading off to the side of the lip but off the front also. That will drive the bait back up, instead of letting it achieve its maximum depth. Most of the baits I have experimented with achieve their maximum depth at a moderate speed."

You can generally over-crank a shallow-running bait because there is not as much surface area on its smaller lip. Plugs with a long, slender lip would be more difficult to over-crank than one with a big, rounded lip, but the latter will go deeper automatically, according to the lure designer.

The water flowing over the lip itself causes a build-up of resistance as the bait slices through the water; that's why all crankbaits pull back. After a certain amount of resistance builds up, it has to unload some way. Then it starts vibrating, dumping off on one side and then the other. That begins the vibration pattern.

"A lot of people don't realize that the lip is just part of the diving plane. That's why you can't take a giant lip and put it on a little bait," explains Sisson. "You must have something for that lip to work against. The back of the lure itself becomes part of the diving plane. A fatter bait has more surface for the lip to work against, and accordingly, will go deeper. A longer bait has similar characteristics."

Some baits are designed to get down deep yet have a small silhouette, somewhere between the injured-minnow type and the fat, diving style. The proper surface area on the back of such lures has to be designed for the bait to get down into the snags. The added area also means more buoyancy to help the lure float up from hang-ups.

Snags And Depths

Anglers know that hang-ups can be a problem, but seldom are more than two or three baits lost to underwater snags in a full day of fishing. Improved versions of 'plug knockers' and heavy line account for the relatively low number. The latter is the key.

A good procedure to follow when initially hung up solid is to 'pop' the line by grabbing it with your hand, stretching it, and then letting go. If the recoil doesn't work, steadily pull it, with rod tip pointed at the snag, to a point just before the breaking strength. Most of the time one of those means will free the plug. The third and final solution is going after it.

A lure has less chance of getting hung up and will reach its maximum depth if it's tuned properly and running straight. Actually, most lures that I have observed run sideways a foot or two, over to one side or the other. That's not to say that a lure that runs off to one side won't catch fish. Sometimes, that's what the fish are looking for.

Any angler who is serious about bass fishing should take his baits to a swimming pool or to any place with clear water where he can watch them run. He needs to make sure that the lures are doing what they are supposed to do.

Because of the lure's pull, many people believe it's going 18 feet deep. But some lures are just hard-pulling lures and they may not be going but a few feet deep.

Crankbaits have been responsible for many huge largemouth. They come in all shapes and colors, but the successful angler must make a selection based on a complete analysis of all existing factors.

The reason is simple. When you pull any lure down, you are pulling a bunch of line down too. The line doesn't go straight from the rod tip to the lure. The line makes a big bow and almost goes straight down near the bait. The heavier the line, the more resistance.

Shake, Rattle, And Roll

"The vibration pattern of a crankbait is what attracts bass," states Sisson. "I think there are several factors that cause a fish to strike; I call them strike stimuli. They feel the vibration pattern a long time before they ever see it," he explains. "That pattern can either turn them on or off. They may watch the bait go by, swim away from it, or be stimulated enough by it to move in for a closer look."

"Built-in rattles and sound chambers only add to the vibration pattern because sound is just vibration, whether it is moving through air or water," explains Sisson. "Shad, crayfish, shrimp and most baitfish makes a high pitch sound. Fishery biologists have described the sound to be similar to the noise given off when two rocks are tapped together underwater."

Any movement through water puts out a vibration pattern. You can pull a piece of line through water and find that out. Some people think light line is best to fish a crankbait with, that the lure will work better and that it will obtain more depth. Sisson believes that to be true, but he also notes that light line also moves less water and thus, makes less noise.

A vibration pattern is the first thing that fish notice, and it either turns them on or off, but the optimal strike-drawing frequency is a hard thing to pinpoint.

"The next stimuli is what I call 'flash patterns'," Sisson says. "It's what attracts the eye of the bass before it really sees the lure. It's the first visual contact with a bait that is moving through the water and throwing off flashes."

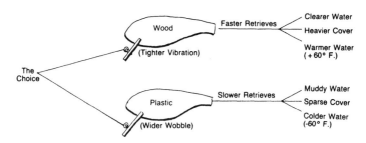

FIGURE 6—*Each crankbait material offers different characteristics. Likewise, their selection for optimal productivity is dependent upon certain existing water conditions.*

Paints have been developed that give off a flash pattern in different colors, not just silver or gold, but in reds and blues, and many crankbait manufacturers are now using them. Chromes and some bright colors like chartreuse seem to put off a glow around the lure.

"The next factor in the fish continuing to strike is the body size and shape of the lure," Sisson says. "What he sees when he gets there is important then. Does the bait really look like something to eat?"

Resemblance to the existing forage is just one of the strike stimuli, but it's important in the overall picture of enticing the fish to take the lure. Silhouette size is a consideration too, throughout the seasons. In the spring, bass will eat little minnows and in the fall, they are used to gorging on bigger forage.

Material Witness

Every material has advantages and disadvantages. Plastic lures are generally easier to manufacture and mass-produce, and there are some excellent plastic baits on the market. You can usually abuse them a little more than you can a balsa wood lure.

One of their chief limitations, though, according to Sisson, is that their density is heavier than water. Air cavities must be built into the plastic lures, and building extremely small lures can often be a problem. Strength cannot be diminished due to the cavities.

"Balsa wood is not as tough, but it's light (density less than water) and you have to add weight to it to get it to do what you want," says Sisson. "Strength must be added to such a soft foundation through the wire harnesses and epoxy glues. The advantages are its flotation, and the ability to put weight where you want to. Balsa is a soft wood that is easily worked."

Foam lures are a lot like balsa in flotation characteristics, according to Sisson. He believes that they are less expensive to manufacture than plastic baits. In making a foam lure, the critical element is metering the foam to get the right amount in the mold.

"A hard wood is midway between a plastic and a balsa in durability and strength," points out Sisson. "It has a strong foundation

The crankbait can resemble just about any forage. When bass are feeding on crayfish, for example, select one that is a clone.

but is still light with a density lighter than water. You don't have to build the strength into it either, like you do balsa. A lure with controlled weight placement is one that will normally run easier, and it is easier to manufacture to control the way the bait swings."

Rattles in baits to add to the vibration were an accident in the beginning, as Sisson tells it. A plastic bait manufacturer was putting weights in his lures and accidentally put small weights (designed for a smaller plug) in a large plug. The manufacturing 'defect' caused a rattling sound, and it also caused a craze! Many good things in this business start off as accidents.

The Final Components

Crankbait hooks should be razor-sharp. You can over-sharpen them only if you make them so thin that the point bends over on the first object you hit. Wise anglers will constantly check the sharpness when pulling on the bait, getting it hung, and digging it through stuff. Be ready, when on the water, to change to the same kind of bait with a fresh set of hooks. Replace old hooks on your baits prior to being on the water.

Rebend a straightened hook only if you are fishing open water. If you are in heavy cover and are having to exert a lot of pressure to 'horse' the fish from the habitat, never reform the hook to its normal shape. Replace the crankbait. Under any circumstances, if you straighten the hooks out very many times, it's best to be thinking about changing them.

The way a lure is put together, e.g. the eye placement in the lip or bait itself, the shape, width, and length of the lip, the hooks, and the body design all come into play. Design or manufacturer inconsistencies in any one of them, though, can throw the lure off.

The eye where the split ring is attached is the key to tuning a lure. Bend it toward the direction that you want the lure to run. A lure can be tuned to run to one side, for example, to bounce around each post in a row of them or to run under a pier. That can be particularly advantageous in the summer when bass are holding tighter to pilings. The result is a lure that resembles a crayfish trying to get on a log.

The depth that a lure runs can be adjusted by making it run sideways. For example, if a lure running true normally obtains eight feet, it can be tuned to run to one side and possibly only get down to four feet. Such a method is productive in shallow water, as long as the lure doesn't achieve what the designers call "critical roll," where the bait will go into a spin.

CHAPTER 3

SLAB STRATEGIES

Count On The Vibrating Baits

THE FIRST STEP to catching bass is finding them. The second step is finding them in a short period of time in order to catch as many as possible. Lure choice, in this situation, is important, and few lures are as consistent for covering a lot of water quickly as vibrating baits.

Call them sonic plugs, slabs or vibrators; it doesn't matter because bass know them well. Many have had one or more of this type lure adorning their lips. The lures all put out a vibrating noise, and bass often react to such a sound with curiosity, approaching vibrations that may resemble hurt forage.

Vibrating baits tend to attract largemouth bass from great distances. Anglers will often go to a slab plug when the chips are down and they need to locate bass fast. The lure's action is extremely good in off-color water as well as clear water, so it can be used anywhere. The plugs will catch fish under just about all conditions.

Randy Fite, a bass guide and tournament pro, effectively uses the baits mostly in shallow waters, seldom those deeper than seven feet. In deeper areas with submerged grass near the surface, though, he'll also select the baits that run very shallow without hard cranking.

Generally, three sizes of vibrating plugs can be found in most manufacturers' lines: a small, medium and large bait. Fite, like most good anglers, prefers the standard or mid-size version of vibrating plug in chrome, gold and, in the late spring, baby bass. He considers that combination extremely effective in the period when winter is on the wane and the bass are just starting to move up from the depths.

"The fish are extremely dormant," points out Fite. "When they are in the depth range of four to seven feet, the lure is a very effective cold water bait."

37

"We use them on Lake Conroe in late February for example," he explains. "An extremely slow retrieve over the shelfs coming off from a submerged point, or in the backs of creeks, work best. The vibrating bait seems to catch fish in those areas better than any other bait."

The vibrating plug has an extremely tight wobble that works effectively at every speed. It will retain its action even at very slow speeds. In cold water, that's particularly important. Once the water temperature reaches 60 degrees, Fite will speed up his retrieve.

Vegetation Factors

The vibrating baits allow anglers to fish vegetation more thoroughly. A spinnerbait or a plastic worm were the lure of choice when fishing around vegetation. A vibrating bait, however, can also work the outer edge of floating plants. Yet when a cast puts the lure in the vegetation, it will still come out of the weeds very freely.

The speed of retrieve controls the depth of the vibrating plugs. Most anglers normally use a steady retrieve, but some try a variety of speeds for maximum bass productivity.

A very effective technique is a retrieve that allows the vibrating lure to hang momentarily in the vegetation. When ripped free, the lure will draw the strikes. If the lure is moving too fast over the weeds without hitting any, it is not nearly as effective.

The hooks on most vibrating plugs don't carry a good reputation. Because the bait is relatively heavy, anglers often lose a high percentage of their fish on vibrating plugs. Some knowledgeable anglers would never consider throwing one without putting more quality treble hooks on the bait, or at least sharpen the existing ones to perfection. Some anglers even go to a slightly larger size in the front, which is the most important hook.

To improve the odds, many will use a soft-action rod and a set the drag on the reel very light. Pressuring a fish will cause it to jump, and with that bait, he has about a 50 percent chance of getting off. A soft-tip rod action plus a fairly light drag setting will allow the fish to swim down, where most bass want to be. That combination makes a big difference in the amount of fish actually put in the boat on vibrating plugs.

The lures are particularly effective over heavy cover, when largemouth are holding on an outside weed line. Emergent sawgrass at the point and scattered submerged pepper grass off the point can be problems for most lures. Billed crankbaits would hit such vegetation after about three cranks and that would be the end of your cast. Even a spinnerbait would probably get its blade fouled or hung up in the grass.

Vibrating baits are responsible for some giant-size bass on occasion, like the author's eight-pounder shown here, although the average catch may be smaller.

About the only kind of lure to toss under those conditions is a vibrating plug that you can just rip out of the pepper grass and continue the retrieve. The vibrating bait could be cast very far to reach schoolers that may come up a little further away.

Feeding Schoolers

Vibrating plugs are good baitfish imitators, and as such, are very effective on bass that are feeding on the major forage, threadfin shad. That means schooling fish.

Just throw it beyond the surface-feeding schools and reel it back fast. That will usually trigger aggressive strikes. Vibrating plugs are excellent around grass because they don't dig down and mire up in the weeds. You can control the depth by holding the rod tip up or down.

Your lure will achieve more depth if you hold the rod in the down position, or keep it high and crank it fast across weedbeds. The lure normally runs true, no matter what the speed of the retrieve. For deep water fishing, the vibrating plug is extremely effective too. You have to know how to work the plugs though.

The plugs sink fairly quickly, reaching that prime mid-depth area where many bass are holding. Let the lure sink to the bottom and then crank it back for maximum action. Or, sometimes fish them deep by pumping them off the bottom.

Activity And Attractions

For best action, vibrating baits should be used with 10 or 12-pound test monofilament line, according to most experts. You get a truer action and more depth out of the plugs and you get more fish strikes.

Larry Nixon often credits his tournament success to vibrating lures. The professional bass angler considers water between 10 and 20 feet as the most effective depth range to pump a vibrating plug along the bottom on structure. His favorite months for employing that particular tactic are August through October.

"The conditions are right when you have located schooling bass along a creek channel and then a cold front hits, driving them away," explains Nixon. "If you can then locate the bass on the bottom, that's when the vibrating plugs will catch them best."

The vibrating plugs will produce best, though, in waters down to 10 feet deep. Fish at that maximum depth will come off the bottom to hit a lure fished above them in six feet, for example. Wisely, good anglers match the size of plug to the size of the baitfish that the bass are feeding on.

"In the early spring, you're looking at tiny shad and bream, so I'll often throw a 1/4-ounce plug," Nixon explains. "I'll throw the mid-range bait a little later in the year, and then in the late summer and fall, I'll throw the 3/4-ounce bait. If I'm fishing for bigger fish, then I'll throw the bigger lure."

His tackle box holds three basic colors of vibrating plugs. He will use a shad imitation such as chrome, a chartreuse with a brown or black back to imitate a bream, and in the spring, he'll use a fluorescent red for a crawfish color.

Sliders And Modifications

Nixon likes the new sliding versions of the Rat-L-Trap and Hot Spot. The line goes through the plug and is attached directly to the treble hook hanging below the belly of the plug. For an angler with a gross of older vibrating baits that he doesn't want to toss, Nixon suggests a modification that will make a standard two-treble plug into a slider.

"Take a pair of needlenose pliers and extract the line tie eye from the lure's back. Then, pull the front hook and eye out of the plug," the professional explains. "Now use an electric drill to make a hole between the two cavities."

"The bit size should be slightly larger than the insert of an ink pen," Nixon explains. "Run the insert through the hole that you drilled into the plug and cut it off flush on each side. Use silicone or epoxy to secure the insert in place."

Nixon then makes a small notch into the bottom of the plug at the insert point, cross-wise to the plug axis. This is done so that the

Open water areas adjacent to deep water and structure of some kind are prime places for tossing slabs. Two bass at a time is not unusual for a couple throwing vibrating baits.

split ring tied directly to the line running through the insert will rest up against the bottom of the plug. The vibrating lure will not always track true unless the notch is sliced correctly, according to the professional. Finally, the rear hook is removed and a large treble hook is attached to the split ring.

The modification does cause the lure to run a little shallower, to about three or four feet in depth. You won't lose as many fish on these "slider" lures, though, since this modification allows the plug body to slide free, up and down the line. The fish has only the treble hook to shake free, and that's much more difficult without the leverage of a heavy bait.

Buying new sliding vibrating plugs or making that one modification to your existing lures may eliminate some bass losses. I am a strong believer in these type of plugs and have found them to be "limit tackle" when employed under many conditions.

Most anyone can catch fish on vibrating plugs. They should be in everyone's tackle box when not hanging from a rod!

CHAPTER 4

SHALLOW WATER WORMIN'

Technique Options For The Plastics

THE WATER COULDN'T have been over four feet deep at the edge of the rushes where Wayne Yohn had just man-handled a 10-pound largemouth. The boat's dash-mounted flasher naturally was full of red blips denoting weeds from the surface on down.

For the bass guide, that fish was nothing for him to really get excited about. He's caught 60 over the 10-pound mark.

Flippin' worms to the shallow "buggy whips" are his forte. Those bullrush clusters surrounded by huge beds of thinner grass vegetation are most productive for the Lakeland, Florida resident. He proved it that day by capturing lunkers of 6 1/2 and 10 pounds. After several photos, both fish were returned to the water by the veteran reed flipper.

"Fish both sides of a clump of reeds," he advises. "I've often fished one side without success, then picked up the bait and dropped it on the other side, where a bass was waiting."

"Always watch the line," he continues, "because the slightest twitch may mean a strike. If that bush shakes when the lure falls to the bottom, chances are that the bass has it, and you can go ahead and set the hook."

"Bass seldom hit the bait on the fall during the spring, though," says the flippin' expert. "They are not actively feeding, so they'll strike the worm as you move it. If the bait drops too fast, it could easily spook them, so lighten up on the sinker."

Yohn's yoyo-type cast in shallow water is, by necessity, smooth and quiet. He will raise the rod tip with the plastic worm just off the water's surface, strip off more line with his left hand, and with an underhand motion, swing the lure in a pendulum motion toward the weed clump. His left hand slows the lure's descent, allowing it to contact the surface noiselessly.

43

"Most of your worm fishing in these thickets is usually with less than 12 feet of line out," says Yohn. "Line control may be the most important key to successful flippin' for anglers just learning this technique."

Jungle Flippin'

In shallow, heavy cover such as bullrushes, Johnson grass, or cattails, Yohn believes strongly in having adequate tackle for the job. His arsenal consists of an eight foot long, heavy action flippin' rod and a spinning reel spooled with 30 pound test monofilament. The experienced bass angler has caught numerous bass using 8-inch black grape worms, adorned with a 5/0 worm hook and 5/8 ounce slip sinker.

The Texas-rigged plastic worm is usually a successful attractor of largemouth. Bass can go wild when fooled by a soft, tasty "morsel."

44

The most productive flippin' pattern during the entire spring period is to work the small bullrush clumps isolated within the emergent grass that abounds on shallow waters. Bigger bass are usually found shallow at this time. The action during the summer will move to the dense buggy-whip patches or grass beds in four or five feet of water. Again, movement in the weeds is an indicator of fish.

The productive flipper will move in tight on the points and pockets and check the water depth and type of bottom present. Bass prefer a clean, sandy bottom, and bullrushes grow in sandy areas.

Yohn has utilized his bullrush worm-flippin' method to achieve great success in tournaments over the past several years. In a one-day "boat" tournament, Yohn and a partner amassed a 60 pound, 2 ounce flippin'-caught string to outfish 142 other competitors. Yohn himself pulled in two largemouth over 10 pounds and several others, including a seven pounder, from the rushes.

Shallow Terrain

Most experienced shallow water worm anglers prefer to flip a bait into bullrushes more than into cattail cover. Rushes are easier to fish because they are straight and rigid. Cattails, which grow in shallower water, have leaves that branch off as the plant rises from the water's surface. Both, however, provide great shallow water cover.

Reeds and cattails that grow in the better areas are taller due to optimal soil conditions. A good sandy soil is more fertile, enhancing vegetation growth. Bass prefer that additional weed cover protection.

Flippin' is extremely effective in some situations, but it is only one of many successful plastic worm techniques applicable to the shallows. Emergent vegetation is usually prominent in shallow waters, allowing such areas to be highly oxygen-enriched and forage-intensive. Many types of aquatic vegetation provide a source of food for predator and prey alike throughout all but the coldest months.

Even in the winter, shallow waters will warm faster and "turn on" quicker with the first hint of spring. Hard bottoms are what attract bedding bass then. Shallows with adequate cover are accessi-

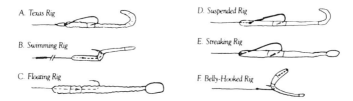

A. Texas Rig

B. Swimming Rig

C. Floating Rig

D. Suspended Rig

E. Streaking Rig

F. Belly-Hooked Rig

FIGURE 7—*The Texas rig, with hook turned back into the worm, is the most versatile. The swimming worm rig spins on the retrieve, while the floating rig uses a buoyant worm worked on top. The suspended rig is for slow work at mid-depths and the streaker for choppy waters. The Belly rig is ideal for milfoil and hydrilla.*

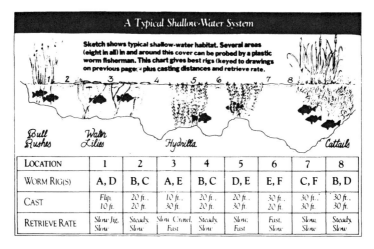

LOCATION	1	2	3	4	5	6	7	8
WORM RIG(S)	A, D	B, C	A, E	B, C	D, E	E, F	C, F	B, D
CAST	Flip, 10 ft.	20 ft., 20 ft.	10 ft., 30 ft.	20 ft., 20 ft.	20 ft., 30 ft.	30 ft., 20 ft.	30 ft., 30 ft.	30 ft., 30 ft.
RETRIEVE RATE	Slow Jig, Slow	Steady, Slow	Slow Crawl, Fast	Steady, Slow	Slow, Fast	Fast, Slow	Slow, Slow	Steady, Slow

FIGURE 8—*Aquatic vegetation holds bass and one or more worm rigs and/or presentations may be employed to attract them. Shown are bullrushes, lily pads, hydrilla and a cattail bog. In selecting a location to fish, the angler should also keep in mind that the bass will be positioned in the shade when possible. During active feeding, bass often relate to edges of cover.*

ble to most worm-tossing anglers too. Even in the thicker, summer mass of milfoil, coontail and hydrilla, the plastics have a place.

The better worming areas are generally where a breakline or change occurs. This might be in the form of a weed-type variance, such as pickerel weed to cattails, or in a small depth change. Bass will hold on a one-foot drop or at the edge between two types of plants. The particular topography would probably dictate the choice of worm rig.

A Texas-rigged worm is productive in shallows that have fairly clean bottoms and vegetation that is rigid and straight. The rig with a 3/0 or 4/0 worm hook turned back into itself to make it weedless, and a bullet-shaped slip sinker on the line in front, is the most popular of all. It is probably also the most versatile.

The sliding weight should be as light as possible in the shallows, particularly around heavy masses of vegetation. A 1/16 or 1/8 ounce sinker is generally ideal for most shallow weed infestations. Casting bulky worms help keep the fare out of bottom cover and in the "strike zone."

Maximizing the catch from certain weed masses in the shallows may require the use of different rigs and presentations. Several surface or near-surface worm rigs may be more effective. The primary idea is to have the plastic bait "make like a snake" swimming through the cover.

Swimming Attractors

Submergent vegetation that grows from the bottom toward the surface may have a "water shelf" just above it. Just a foot or two between the surface and the weed bed is sufficient to work either a "swimming worm" or floating worm rig across a shallow expanse without fear of getting entangled. Both rigs sport exposed hooks that would make them less appropriate for other shallow habitat.

The swimming worm rig has been deadly in protected waters among vegetation beds and along defined banks for about 20 years. The kinky-shaped rig utilizes a No. 1 straight-shank hook threaded a third of the way into the head of a straight-tail worm. Only the hook's barb is brought out, leaving the worm with a bend in it. A black swivel is tied about 12 inches in front of the worm to prevent line twist as the lure twirls through the water.

Purple with glo-pink tail is a hard color combination to beat. The swivel, hook and six-inch worm provide the only weight for casting purposes. For the spinning gear to achieve a steady retrieve back to the boat, that's sufficient. Small canal and pond bass will literally eat this up. The exposed hook allows for an easy hook set and the weightlessness entices the bass to hold onto the lure longer.

I first used this rig on an ultralight outfit along a mile-long canal. The water sloped gradually from the bank past sparse aquatic weeds to a depth of only five feet or so. Most of the 15 largemouth that I caught and released were in about two feet of water waiting for a slow-moving morsel to swim by.

Floating And Belly-Hooked Models

The floating worm rig encompasses a highly buoyant worm along with a light, gold-plated wire hook in a 2/0 or 3/0 size. A long, 8 to 10-inch fat body worm with paddle tail is probably optimum for flotation. The hook, positioned one third of the way down

The swimming worm rig fished in the shallow vegetation of canals and streams is responsible for more bass than any other artificial lure.

the worm's body is light weight, which allows the rig to be twitched along the surface over grass beds in slow jerks.

The rig can be snaked slowly across the surface and stopped periodically to lie motionless. When fishing extremely heavy cover, the hook can be embedded in the worm Texas-style. A foam snake head can be added to the rig to help its flotation. It's easy to see the strike on this rig in most situations and that's exciting. A surface explosion will long be remembered.

Another rig that draws a lot of attention from largemouth inhabiting hydrilla and milfoil expanses is a belly-hooked worm. The six-inch straight worm is simply fished with the exposed 3/0 hook through the mid-section, sans weight.

When fishing any of the worm rigs described, the shallow water angler should keep his rod tip high. The hits can be more easily seen and felt, and slack can be quickly given if needed. When a worm temporarily hangs on a weed and then comes free, slack can be given. The descending bait is more susceptible to attacks.

A weedless worm rig that sinks into pockets in the vegetation will be an effective one. With most shallow worm rigs, the bait can be slowed considerably to entice a "follower" or one of the more deliberate lunkers that swim shallow, weed infested waters.

As soon as the shallow water temperatures warm to 55 degrees, there's a worm rig that will produce. Most of the possibilities are exciting to fish. What's better—they catch bass.

CHAPTER 5

WORMING SPEED VARIATIONS

Slow And Fast Ways To Lure Bass

BASS ARE FINICKY eaters during their spawning activities, so careful attention to fishing techniques, particularly the speed of retrieve, is justified for successful angling. At other times of the year, a lightning fast retrieve may be necessary for maximum action.

The secret of a few productive anglers for many years, 'dead worming' is one technique that was developed and refined for use only during an eight-week period in the spring. The 'dead worm' method that's slowly being revealed to the majority of bass anglers may be the most productive way to entice a spawning or post-spawn bass to a hook-up. It does take a lot of patience, though, and a lot of finesse.

Fishing a 'dead worm' requires an angler to remain alert, with fingers sensitive to the lightest pick up. Spring time bass on the bed, or just coming off it, will seldom spend energy to charge the plastic wiggler. They will, however, mouth the bait gently as they pick it up to remove it, and that movement through the rod must be felt by the angler.

Most anglers experience the occasional soft 'tap' action with the more conventional 'hop-skip' worm fishing techniques. 'Dead worming,' however, is a technique that motivates spring bass to act. Coupled with a salt-impregnated worm, the system is the key to ending the short-strike syndrome exhibited by bedding and post-spawn largemouth everywhere.

To fish plastic worms successfully using the 'dead worm' technique, anglers must become line watchers. Sensitivity to a soft touch by an eight-pound bass, versus bumping or nudging an underwater structure, is vital. The plastic lure must drop freely on a semi-taut line, slowly gliding downward rather than plummeting.

51

Careful observation of the line should help detect any twitch or sideways movement. The line should be slack once the worm reaches

Successful anglers, like the author who's trying to keep warm here, are using the salt-impregnated worms fished 'dead' to take several cool-weather lunker bass.

the bottom. Let the worm settle to the bottom and rest there for at least half a minute.

Then, very slowly, lower the rod and take in most of the slack while leaving a slight bow in the line. This will allow any critical movement to be seen without the bass getting suspicious. The rod tip should be pointing at about 60 degrees above the water's surface and directly in front of you for best detection of any resistance.

Retrieve Reasoning

Now, for the retrieve. Nothing is more important in successful 'dead worming' than the retrieve. Concentrate on the proper slow speed and depth control of the bait, or you might as well forget it. Spring bass full of roe are exhausted after the spawning "ordeal;" they move slow and are sluggish, and so must be the movements of the bait.

With this technique and at this time of year, it is very easy to fish too fast. The worm must be 'inched' with a series of light pulls and pauses.

As the worm slowly moves, pause the retrieve. The bait shouldn't drop off any underwater structure for maximum effect. During the retrieve, pause for at least five seconds and let the worm sit. A s-l-o-w retrieve is the key.

Observe the line, and 'feel' the bass habitat as the bait "snails" its way through vegetation and other bottom structure. It's a waiting game, but if retrieved properly, the bass will often pick the worm up after several seconds of "dead" action. Bass are particularly curious in the spring. The largemouth must have plenty of time to inspect the offering and move into position to react to it.

On a clear, spring day several years ago, I found this technique to be most effective. The canal on which I slowly floated down had numerous beds along its bank. On my first cast to the shore, my worm landed on the grassy bank. I crawled the bait into the shallows and immediately saw a boil.

I quickly set the hook. A seven pound, spawning female erupted on the surface trying to spit out the seemingly half-dead morsel that fooled her.

Even in the spring, when bass concentrate their energy on bedding, they don't give up without a fight. I struggled to force her out of a nearby submerged tree and, finally, into the net. Always in favor of conservation, particularly at this time of the year, I gained further satisfaction by releasing the trophy.

Canal Bank Variation

I've often found that the shallow canals off deep water are sometimes loaded with bass. A fairly successful technique involving a variation of the dead worm rigged self-weedless can be used successfully for these canal fish. The technique is most effective using a salt-impregnated worm.

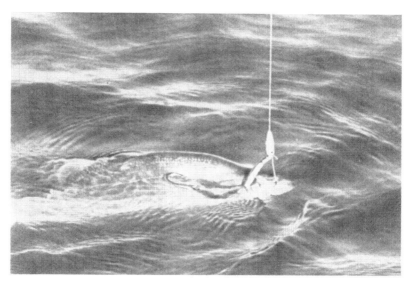

Spring-time bass just won't let go of a salt worm, according to many. It is as close to edible as an artificial can be.

Again, the slow speed of the worm action is the key. After casting it up on the bank, the plastic bait is allowed to sit for a minute or more without letting the line hit the water's surface.

Then, slowly crawl the scented wiggler into the water, where the weight of the hook lets it fall. The worm should sit still in six to 12 inches of water at the canal bank for at least half a minute. Soon, a bass will approach and the worm will simply be inhaled.

On one fishing trip to a nearby canal, I caught and released more than 20 bass weighing over five pounds each using this unique approach. By using this technique, I found fishing during the spawning period to be more consistent and successful.

Rigging For Slow Going

I prefer to 'dead worm' with a Texas-style rig and a 4/0 worm hook anchored with a 1/8 or 1/16 ounce bullet sinker. Line testing 14 to 17 pounds allows for better buoyancy and water drag than lighter lines, and they provide a softer approach to an observant bass.

Line size can be decreased when fishing areas with little cover, in clear water or for bass weighing no more than seven or eight pounds. Whatever the line, however, keep in mind that the slower a worm descends to the bottom, the better the chances of a bass mouthing it. Similarly, the slower it crawls on the bottom, the better the chances of a strike. Additionally, sharp hooks are equally vital to angler success.

Figuring out bedding and post-spawn bass is not easy, although they are easier to catch in a pre-spawn period. Individual clean-sand bass beds on flats indicate the season has begun. Other sure signs of spawning bass are a pH approaching 7.4, water temperature readings in the mid 60's, and numerous big bass that will not strike.

Releasing any fish caught is the best mode of operation during this time of year. For bass experiencing the spring doldrums, 'dead worming' should motivate them to action. Patient anglers will soon find results on their line.

Suspending Or Streaking

A strike on extremely slow- or fast-moving worm rigs can occur any time, even next to the boat. The self-weedless "suspended" worm is another slow version that is gently twitched along through heavy emergent cover or just under floating cover, like duck weed. A 3/0 or 4/0 Tru-Turn Brute hook is turned into an eight-inch worm to provide the rig neutral buoyancy. No weight is added.

In sparse vegetation, the hook point can be left exposed without too much fear of entanglements. The rig can be worked from just below the surface down toward the bottom, depending on how it is retrieved. Strikes on the slow wiggling bait will usually be premeditated and, in shallow water, observable.

A friend and I first tried the "streaking worm" retrieve several years ago in gale force winds. A shallow point in the small reservoir sported white caps . . . and bass. We initially had a largemouth slam a Texas-rigged worm as it was being quickly reeled (buzzed) to the boat. A few minutes later, that happened again, so we began using the "quick" retrieve on each cast.

We eventually took off the bullet weight, since we needed none to cast 40 yards with the wind. Our worms were 8 and 9- inches in length, ideal for casting without a sinker and for attracting attention as they made their way across a choppy surface. The 18 or so bass that exploded on the fast-retrieved offerings were chunky, up to seven pounds.

I've often used the streaking worm method over windy shallows and it remains effective. It's particularly productive over submergent vegetation that does not encroach upon the surface. A 4/0 or 5/0 worm hook will handle most strikes. A slight pause is generally advantageous before the hook set. Too quick a set can result in a lost fish. Largemouth on a shallow wind-blown bar or point are active, feeding fish, so the strikes will always be exciting.

Slow Night Action

Don't put up the plastic wigglers when the sun goes down. Bass move en masse to the shallows after dark to feed and most anglers would be surprised at the worm action available then.

Bass during the six-week stretch known as "lockjaw" time, can often be caught by "dead worming" the shallows. The worm should be fished dead in the water in the quiet reaches.

Some tips may help. Darker hues of plastic such as black, purple or blue-grape offer a more distinct silhouette which will help the bass "home in" on the target. Fatter worms fished on the surface present more bulk to the larger predators below, resulting in more interest from them.

If you can get away with a faster retrieve, imitation snakes and eels offer maximum tail action. Paddle tails and curl-tail type worms and eels send off the vibrations only if moved. Slow, steady retrieves, however, usually offer maximum action. The fare is easier for the bass to find.

Use short casts and stay alert. Lure presentation, control and observation (or feel) will be enhanced, resulting in fewer strikes missed. Bullet-shaped rattle floats and weights, light stick additives and glowing plastics are the latest wiggle in night worming and they are productive.

Try some of the slow retrieves or the lightning fast ones to increase results. Fast rigs are fun and sometimes productive; slow ones are usually more successful, but it's all in the timing.

CHAPTER 6

JIGGING VARIABLES

Techniques, Trailers, Weights And Hooks

THE MOST OVERLOOKED, yet productive, lure of modern times may just be the jig. In the 1950s and early '60s, its reign was supreme. Then other types of bait began grabbing the imagination of the angling crowd. The jig however, continued to catch fish.

The bait in its "early years" was treated as a northern bass lure, or one exclusively for cold weather. In the last 10 years, however, it has become known as a year-round bait, thanks in part to the flippin' technique. Today, the new technology that has aided jig fishermen is at work more than ever. Improvements in jig head design, skirt material and weed guards have been dramatic.

Naturally, the jig and trailer most resembles a crayfish or, in some cases, a small snake. To that end, most jig and trailer manufacturers offer brown, black and crayfish colors. There are many makers of dark-colored jigs today, Stanley Jigs and Arkie Lures being probably the better known of the lot. Knight Manufacturing, Whing Ding Lure Company, Eagle Lures, Strike King Lures, Anglers Pro Specialties, Cotee Bait Company, Fishin' Worm Company and a host of others also make bass jigs.

Bait Sizing

Larry Nixon has relied on jigs heavily in his successful tournament accomplishments. The Toledo Bend guide, and one of the top performers of the touring bass men, feels that the weight of the jig is an important consideration. The head size that Nixon selects will depend on the water conditions more than anything else.

Fish will react the same way in very hot water as they do in very cold water. Extreme temperatures make them sluggish. It then takes a little slower-falling lure to make a bass strike.

When the water is below 60 degrees, Nixon will normally throw a 3/8-ounce (or lighter) bait. The fish's metabolism in cold water has slowed considerably, and Nixon feels that the bait should be slowed down accordingly. The lighter baits will accomplish that job and net more strikes.

Dense stands of vegetation attract big largemouth and the successful angler will often employ a jig-and-eel combo.

Between 60 and 75 degrees, the bass will still hit the smaller bait, but the pro will often go to a heavier jig. Nixon feels that he can cover a little more water with a one-half ounce jig and that his casts are more accurate.

If the wind is blowing, naturally you are going to have to use a heavier bait. That helps keep the jig on the bottom within the strike zone longer.

Then, at some point between 70 and 80 degrees, the fish will sometimes stop hitting most jigs, according to Nixon. They've seen a lot of jigs thrown at them throughout the spring. The angler should then go to a very heavy jig, a half-ounce or 9/16-ounce to get a "fast sink." That should trigger strikes.

Hook Happenings

There are a variety of hook shapes and sizes donning lead heads today and the angler certainly has a choice with regard to them. Stanley makes jigs with a flippin' hook or a casting hook, and the former are used by anglers primarily when flippin' brush or shallow water structure in waters less than 10 feet deep.

When an angler is using 10 to 17-pound test line and a medium-heavy action rod, he should stay with the casting-size hook. Stanley's 3/0 casting hook is a smaller diameter hook than their "flippin' hook." It penetrates well.

"So many times you don't feel strikes on a jig," says Nixon. "You more or less pick up on it and there's something there. Then you realize that it's a fish and you don't get a real good hook set. With the smaller diameter casting hook," he explains, "you don't need a great hook set."

Trailer Thoughts

A pig trailer is employed by Nixon about 80 percent of the time. Anytime the water temperature is less than 68 degrees, Nixon will normally use the pork. Most anglers seldom feel the fish hit a jig because the strike occurs on the fall so much of the time.

A variety of hooks and trailers can be used to entice jig-attracted bass.

"Even on the cast, they'll hit it going down," explains Nixon. "With pork, they get a better bite and hold onto the bait longer."

There are three Uncle Josh porks that work well on jigs, according to Nixon. The No. 11 frog is a smaller, more compact bait suitable for fishing in waters that may have smaller bass in the one to two-pound range. The No. 1 frog can be used when flippin' for large bass with a long rod and heavy jig. The 800 spring lizard is also a good choice when looking for big bass; it provides a little bit more bulk without being too long.

When using pork as a trailer, experienced anglers often take a 1/4-inch long piece of plastic worm and slip it up on the hook to keep the pork from rolling back.

In the hands of an angler with confidence in it, the jig and pig is a deadly bait. Nixon likes to use it about 80 percent of the time, for cooler water conditions and larger fish. The other 20 percent of the time, he chooses the Stanley 4-inch crawworm that comes packaged with the jigs for the trailer addition.

"If I could use plastic all of the time and get away with it, I probably would," he says. "Usually, I'll stick with a black or brown crawworm with a little tint to the claws, such as fire or blue."

Colorful Combinations

The trailer chosen is generally the same color as the jig, and the same criteria applies. Off-colored water dictates a black or dark

The shallow flats offer various types of topography in which to work a jig. The baits will work year around.

63

trailer. If the water is clear, see-through colors are preferred. As is often the case with any lure, trailer color choice is often based on a confidence factor beyond the water color.

Nixon's color choice for the jig, however, is normally determined by the water color. In darker colored water, he'll either use a black jig or one with a fluorescent tip, such as a fire tail or chartreuse tail. That gives a little more color and makes the bait a little more visible to the fish.

"I like the contrast of the two-tone jig skirts," says Nixon. "They are the greatest things that ever happened to jig fishing. You now have the metal flake colors, that work so well on the worm, available on a jig!"

Crayfish are normally darker in color in the darker water and that's one reason why many anglers prefer a dark-colored jig. The visibilities in dark or off-color waters are such that you can only see down 18 inches from the surface. In waters with clarities of four or five feet, a brown jig or one of the new flake colors will give more flash and should work extremely well.

Summer Locals

Heavy cover is the best area in which to use jigs during the hot weather. It's a time when you have to put the bait right in front of the fish. It takes the right cast into a brush pile or grass bed to attract the strike.

Boat docks, pilings, logs, etc. are prime summer time targets, and in the hot weather, casts should be extremely short. The real key for summer time jig angling success, though, is making a good presentation. You have to put it right on top of the fish because they are not really feeding; they are more or less guarding their territory.

Many bass professionals feel the jig is a dependable bait that they can usually call upon year-round to catch fish. I've found the same to be true. In my estimation, it deserves much more credit than it usually gets. It's a winner!

CHAPTER 7

SKIPPIN' AND BUZZIN' BAITS

Heavy-Cover Methods For Pre-Spawners

"IT'S LIKE SEEING a country side full of deer, yet when the deer hunting season opens, we think all the deer have left," says Ron Shearer. "That's generally not the case, though. They just lay down and are very still while we hunt right over them."

"Fishing during a pre-spawn condition is actually like hunting, only it's in water. The key is to hunt the fish and find out how to make them bite," explains Shearer. "Finding the proper depth, lure and retrieve speed are the parameters."

He has fashioned a very effective technique for catching bass under active pre-spawn conditions. The bearded angler calls it 'skippin', and he has used it over many years on lakes throughout the country.

Pre-spawn bass are edgy. When the water first warms up ten degrees or so, the cautious fish start moving into shallower water. That's true nationwide. Whether it's an ice-covered northern lake or a 50 degree lake in Florida, it's that ten degree change that puts them on the move.

Under those conditions, when the bass first come up, they're a little bit leery being in shallower water with increasing fishing pressure. The normal spring fishing fever and boats running around the lake will cause bass there to respond differently.

Shearer was about eight years old and growing up on the Kentucky River when he first noticed that literally hundreds of bass were laying underneath the overhanging willow tree branches. He fashioned an outfit from a cane pole and a taped-on push button reel, which he soon learned was the answer to skipping a bait back to the fish. He would cast side arm with a golf club-type swing and skip a plastic worm back underneath the willow limbs to catch numerous bass. The worm would skip like a rock over the surface. Shearer continued this effective 'skippin' method throughout his childhood.

When he turned to professional angling, the young angler began practicing with most lure types and spent several days with each until he felt he had become proficient with as many lure techniques as possible. Developing confidence took hour after hour, and day after day of practicing until Shearer finally felt he could compete in national bass tournaments. Yet, he knew that each angler usually has one unique method that he draws upon, under special circumstances. His was the 'skippin' that he had learned as a kid.

The easy-going Kentuckian never thought much about it until 1977, when he used a 7 1/2 foot spinning rod to win a national bass tournament on Kentucky Lake. He employed a swift side arm cast to skip the plastic worm and pegged slip sinker under overhanging branches.

Shad Flippin'

"You have to drive it way back into the bushes," says Shearer. "It's just like skipping a rock across the water. This is most effective when the fish are too spooky to flip. The worm or jig going across the water looks like a shad flipping across the surface. I've had a lot of bass hit it like a buzz bait."

"The bigger fish are often back in the willow trees, but if you get up close to flip them, you may spook the fish," he says. "So, just back off and make a two-handed swing with the long spinning outfit. The spinning reel sometimes has its drawbacks, but for this method, it can't be topped."

On Sam Rayburn Lake in Texas, he stayed far away from the willow trees and skipped a jig through them. The bass would hit the lure deep in the trees, and it was difficult to get them out. So Shearer tried 'burning' the lure out to the edge of the brush and then letting the jig fall. That technique worked and he landed several that struck the lure at the cover's edge.

"They're like little dogs," explains Shearer. "They get curious and follow it to the edge, where they would hit it."

The skippin' lure that Shearer prefers is a 5/16 ounce jig with a flippin' hook in it. He adorns his jig with a piece of pork frog to make it fall slower. That trailer also helps prevent hangups in the heavy cover being fished.

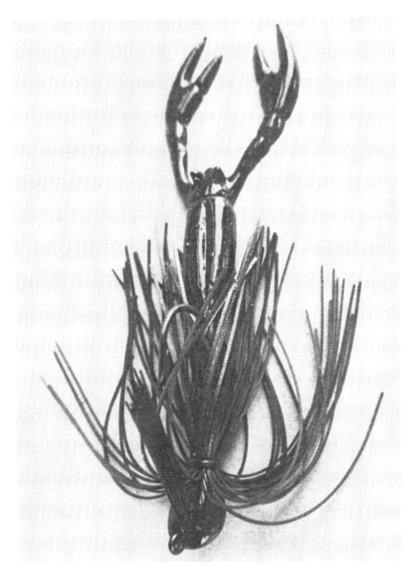

The jig fished by skippin' is a most effective bait when in the hands of an angler with confidence in his casting abilities.

Buzz Spoon

A similar method that works for Shearer during spring on waters with heavy vegetation involves a modified spoon. He'll add a buzz bait blade in front of it and work it fast over heavy cover, pausing to let it fall into oft-times productive holes and pockets.

"You have the best of both worlds. With the in-line buzz blade, it'll buzz right across the top of the grass," says Shearer. "When you get to the holes, you can slow it down to wobble just like a spoon."

That's very effective if the buzz blade and spoon are properly matched. The interaction between the two of them has to be right, as do the conditions. Cloud cover is the optimal sky condition on most lakes, and dense vegetation is the preferred terrain.

Grass beds with isolated holes are best for using this lure combination. The regular in-line buzz bait will run through this kind of cover well, but will not easily attract a bass if you drop it into a hole. Most in-line buzz baits do not resemble forage once you stop them.

"A spoon will wobble down if you drop it into a hole. This combination falls just like a spoon," says Shearer. "You can wobble the bait slowly through the hole and then break out on top and buzz it on to the next hole."

The largest bass Shearer ever caught on the rig was a 13 pounder from Florida's St. Johns River in 1974.

Timbered shorelines exist in many areas around the country, and such areas can be effectively fished with skippin' jigs and buzz baits.

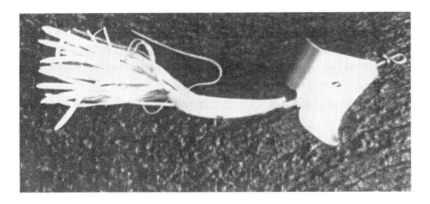

In-line buzz spoons worked near-surface can produce a lot of excitement in the weedy shallows. Points, pockets and "holes" in the grass should be carefully fished for maximum results.

"I could stand and hold the fish up and its tail would turn out on the side of my boat. I've never seen such a bass!" claims Shearer, who released the monster.

Adaptation

Not all of Shearer's buzzing pays off, but the angler can, like the spring bass he's chasing, adapt. When the pre-spawners are overly cautious about buzz baits, this bass angler can usually catch one. On a trip one April morning, he found the sun high and the bass not interested in feeding on the surface. He was after some impulse strikes from beneath lay-down logs.

He cast the bait and was running in along the floating log when he noticed the tail of a good-sized fish on the opposite side. On the following cast, the bass swam over, looked at Shearer's buzz bait, and stopped right beside the log, just eight feet from the boat. The bass could see the angler and vice-versa.

Shearer threw the bait back several times, but the fish just wouldn't hit it. Not giving up, he noticed a little shelf on the log's submerged portion and threw the buzz bait back to let it fall right down onto the lip. The bass then swam up to nose the bait, and nibbled at the blade a couple of times.

The bass wouldn't get near the skirt and hidden hook, so Shearer kept shaking the rod tip to twitch the lure enticingly. Finally, though, the buzz bait rolled over and the hook became embedded in the stump. The now anchored lure was affixed to the log, and the largemouth of about three pounds was "on point" at the buzz bait.

By now, the boat was only five feet away, so he quickly broke his line and threw a plastic worm to the fish. The largemouth swam over to the worm, looked at it, and then swam back to point the buzz bait. Shearer sprayed his worm with a fish attractant and tossed it back to the bass. It promptly repeated the previous scenario, only this time it swam much closer to the smell-enhanced worm. Four more times he cast, but the fish just wouldn't have anything to do with the lure.

Finally, he let the worm fall to the lip of the stump, near where the bass, just like a fine hunting dog, was still pointing the white-skirted lure. Shearer twitched the worm a few times and the bass would swim toward it and stop. As he reeled in, he happened to glance back and noticed the bass was still hitting at the buzz bait's skirt.

Shearer watched the bass hit at the snagged buzz bait five more times before it dawned on him what to do. He cast the worm to the log and worked it right up into the skirt of the buzz bait. He just let the worm lay there in its newfound 'hideaway'. A gentle twitch of the rod tip made the worm shake and the skirt move. That enticed the bass to suck the skirt in once again, but it got the worm instead. Shearer's persistence paid off!

When fish are skitterish, offer them a buzz spoon or skippin' jig. If they don't work, then adapt!

CHAPTER 8

SURFACE LURE ACTION

Walkin' Over The Weedbeds

SURFACE-BUZZING spinnerbaits are among the hottest bass lures on the market today. The lures generally have a blade design that pops them up on the surface and allows the fisherman to crank them back at a very slow pace, on top at all times.

Probably the bait that can be moved the slowest is Norman's Triple Buzz, a three-bladed buzzer that sprays water above the surface even at the slowest speeds. Used around dense grass patches such as pepper grass, sawgrass and eel grass, buzz baits are normally fished with the rod tip held high. The angler should begin reeling just before the lure hits the water so that it is on the surface.

Buzz baits are effective in both pockets and on the point of weed beds, according to Tampa marine dealer, Jack Westberry. He has fished waters all over the country and often chooses a buzzer. The retrieve should usually be slow, but can be speeded up to trigger bass into striking.

"Two elements make the baits successful," says the former college professor. "Noise and contact. The lures must be emitting sound and be making contact with the cover where bass may be living."

When we have fished together, I have marveled at his keeping the buzz bait in contact with structure. The strikes would occur just after the lure had bumped the piece of structure above the bass. Explosions then were exciting.

Torque Movements

Different buzz baits move in different retrieval trajectories. Some with two blades, such as the popular Lunker Lure, moves to the left as it approaches the angler, while the Triple Buzz moves to the right while being retrieved. The turning of the blade provides a 'torque' of sorts that causes the lure to move off the course.

This is good news to an angler wanting to fish a particular side of cover. He can select a buzz bait that runs to the right and fish it in front of cover to his left as the boat moves forward. That lure should always return to make contact with the cover. An angler in the back of the boat may want to throw a buzz bait which exhibits a reverse torque so that he can more effectively work the other side of the cover.

Sound is especially important in stained or roily waters, since visibility could be minimal. The main attractor under these conditions requires the right sound.

In tuning the lures, often the more used or worn the lure, the better sound that it produces. So, to break them in, some anglers stick their rod tips with buzzers attached out of the window on the way to the lake and let the blade revolve a few thousand times.

Surface Excitement

Casting some lures into the trenches of vegetation found on most lakes may, in fact, be an exercise in futility. Baits not up to the challenge will often force an angler to make excuses for a less than successful day. Dense weed cover fishing in shallow water can be most effective with surface lures or top water baits.

In waters less than five feet deep, surface baits are effective around the heavy weed cover. To entice a lunker bass to come up like thunder and murder a bait on the surface is an exciting feat. Often, bass may be on the feed, while at other times it may be necessary to excite the fish into striking.

Actually, little movement is required to disturb the surface and produce some audible noise. Bass in the shade and concealment of submerged or emergent weed bed will usually note the action above them. Many of the favorite heavy weed cover baits do not float and will descend to the bottom if the line becomes slack. Since the action and control of these lures is through the rod tip, a taut line is a must.

A surface-worked lure will bring the bass to the top, making it easier to keep the bass head up and out of the entanglements below.

Keeping big bass on the surface and out of trouble is the key to landing them in heavy cover. A surface-worked lure in heavy weed cover will bring the bass to the top, making it easier for the angler to keep the bass head up and out of entanglements below. That doesn't always work, but it's a good bet.

Entanglements

A friend and I were on the St. Johns River just above Lake George one day when the weather was brutally cold. We selected surface spoons and were tossing them in the shallow coves that appeared weed-laden. Some coves were only two feet deep and one such area had a long stretch of entanglements in the shallows.

My partner's cast to the left side of the submerged weed mass brought an instant strike, but before he could force the fish from the inundated cover, it had become entangled. The seven pound largemouth had smashed the topwater spoon and dove into the tangles.

We quickly worked the boat over to the obstruction, to where the fish was trying to break off. Our anxiety was short-lived, however, as

I grabbed the weed entanglement and gently lifted the whole mess to the surface. I slid the net under the fish.

I unhooked the bass and handed it to my friend for admiring prior to its release. Meanwhile, I worked on freeing the lure and line from the entanglement. In a situation like that, there wasn't much that he could do to power the fish from the shallow structure.

Big largemouth seem to know when they have the protection needed to escape potential predators, like us anglers. They feed in areas that provide maximum cover and entanglements, and the surface bait is an ideal lure to get at them. The Weed Walkers and their predecessors (without the paddle wheel blade) have been a favorite of mine for use in such areas for years.

Following Wakes

In waters with heavy weed growth, a fast-moving bait is natural on the surface. A second wake can often be seen forming behind the first. Simply keep it coming fast enough to keep the propeller, spinner or turn wheel turning on or just under the surface and be ready to set the hook.

Guiding a lure through a bed of lily pads or other emergent vegetation takes practice; watching the line, as well as the lure, is important to prevent snags and have proper control of the bait. Short casts are most practical, and boat movement should be minimal to prevent hangups.

Casts should be made ahead of the boat as the angler works the fringes of the bonnets so that the line of retrieve will not loop behind the boat. A more taut line means better lure control and a better hook set when needed. A productive skitter, spoon- type plug rides the water surface in a twitching pattern. The weedless lure can ride up and over pads as no other lure can.

A big bass is particularly hard to land from a pad jungle, but having a lure that will work well in the bonnets and provoke the strike is the major consideration. In a thick pad bed with just a few small openings of water, bass will have little time to focus on the lure and will strike instinctively, at times even missing the lure. When they do take it solidly, some fish may be lost trying to get them out of the entanglements.

Weeds that grow to the surface of a lake and then mat up and clog the water, are particularly hard to fish. Many southeastern lakes are full of hydrilla. Many varieties of small floating plants that also cover the surface require a special type of lure. To be an effective producer in this type of cover, a lure must ride the surface easily over any growth of aquatic plants.

For areas such as these, again the paddle-wheel type spoon has the ability to ride the surface and hop over small obstructions. The retrieve is started just before the lure lands on the water. Most of these baits ride on their backs with the hook riding up, away from the vegetation. Large bass are excited by the dancing bait and explode the surface to get a piece of it.

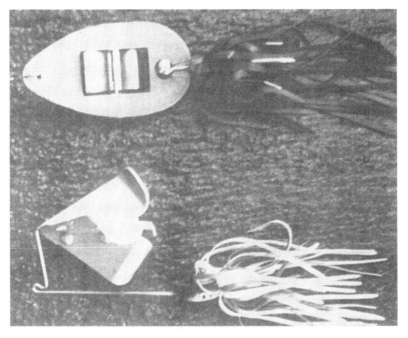

Dense weed cover fishing in shallow water can be most effective with surface spoons or buzzing spinner baits. The blade designs allows the fisherman to crank them back slowly keeping the baits on top at all times.

Monster Bait

"Bass will follow this type of lure for 20 feet in heavy weeds before pouncing on it," notes Buddy Wright, of Jacksonville, Florida. "When a second wake forms behind the first, the trick is to just keep the retrieve coming and be ready."

Wright's cast to long-stemmed eel grass late last April was pounced on by a St. Johns River bass of large proportions. The monster came out of the stringy vegetation below the boat to grab a Weed Walker spoon. Wright kept steady pressure on the fish, but he could feel the fish's efforts to burrow deeper into the entanglement. Fishing alone, he had few options other than to keep pressuring the fish to back out of its 'hole.'

The giant largemouth finally emerged from the shallow grass with weed adornment and was landed. It weighed 18 pounds, 13 ounces and appears to be the third largest bass ever taken from Florida waters. The fish was 29 1/2 inches long with a 26 1/2 inch girth.

We won't all catch monster bass on our surface offerings, but knowing the lures to use in shallow cover and successful ways to fish them is vital to success.

CHAPTER 9

SPINNERBAIT TACTICS

Blade Technology And Productivity

THE SPINNERBAIT NEVER really gained respect until Ken Cook, a fisheries biologist/turned professional angler from Elgin, Oklahoma, used one to win $100,000 in a 1983 bass tournament. He tossed a 24 kt "Gold Eagle" spinnerbait to amass over 41 pounds of bass in the four day event.

Cook and 258 other professional anglers battled a March cold front with unseasonable winds gusting to 50 miles per hour and cold water temperatures in an attempt to win the giant jackpot. Cook was one of a few that caught fish each day. Since then, the spinnerbait has received a lot more recognition and fish-catching respect.

Cook has caught many bass since on the same bait, and has even relied on a modification during tough times. In one tournament, he had located bass in thick brushy tree tops in 10 to 15 feet of water. The fish were holding six feet deep in the thickest tangles.

He modified the heavy Gold Eagle (1/2 oz.) spinnerbait by replacing the standard #6 blade with a smaller #4 Colorado blade. This allowed the lure to fall easier and faster into the thick limb cover, making for a more efficient presentation. Most bass hit the lure after it fell off a limb.

"I further enhanced the vibration produced by the blade by flattening it out somewhat with a pair of pliers," says Cook. "A flatter blade vibrates more than a deeply cupped blade of similar size," he explains. "This gave a 'hard' vibration which attracted the strike better, without producing the excessive water resistance which would keep the bait from falling as quickly."

Cook won that tournament with 15 bass that weighed 45-pounds, 13-ounces.

The state of the art regarding spinnerbaits has progressed more rapidly than many other lure technologies. Today's anglers are able to toss spinnerbaits with bass bearing swivels attached to blades of various sizes. Some are size and shape-adjustable, some have a rotating blade nearest the head and others have thin wire shafts that enhance the spinner vibrations. Some even have an upper shaft that pivots back out of the way of a strike. And, the innovations have yet to cease.

Speed Considerations

Many anglers today count upon the spinnerbait in many situations. They are effective and easy to handle under most conditions. Best of all, they are a fast bait which can be used to quickly eliminate water and find fish, a characteristic valued by the pros, like Cook and Rick Clunn.

Some of Clunn's biggest bass were caught on spinnerbaits. In fact, the professional angler opts for one when after a big fish.

The spinnerbait is one of the most productive baits of all times. In the hands of a good angler, the lure will attract bass.

"I used Stanley's 1/2-ounce spinnerbait with transparent skirt at Lake Meade in a major bass contest. The head design allows it to come though the thickest cover," he says, "because that's where you normally want to throw a spinnerbait. It should be making contact with the cover."

That lure was responsible for his impressive victory with a different technique, however, one that he has used for many years in clearer, warm water. The spinnerbait can be ripped at maximum speed for maximum production under such circumstances. It won't roll or turn over on its side either, according to Clunn.

In the old days, spinnerbaits were built differently. In one tournament, for example, he even added a 1/2 ounce rubber- core sinker to the spinnerbait. That very effective rig helped to keel the bait during a fast retrieve.

He was rippin' (rapidly retrieving) the bait across the surface of the water over huge beds of milfoil. The bass would wait until it got half way back to the boat and then they would slam the spinnerbait. He caught several bass in the four, five and six-pound range that day and won a major bass championship.

Clunn used the extra-weight trick for many years and still does, when needed. Often, he has taken a 1/2-ounce spinnerbait and added another 1/4 to 1/2-ounce rubber-core sinker to the blade shaft.

Size Considerations

Most anglers naturally have ideas regarding the best spinnerbait size to use. The proper selection should depend on what the angler is trying to accomplish; typical size of fish, water conditions, etc. Spinnerbaits come in a variety of sizes, and there should be one in your Plano that's appropriate for the given conditions.

Size of lure should be dictated by the size of the forage that the fish are feeding on, and to some extent by the average size of bass present in the water being fished. You should try to determine that, regardless of how difficult it may be.

"In clear water conditions, I would probably go with a 1/8-ounce spinnerbait," he says. "Where bass grow bigger, I'll use a

Heavy cover is where spinnerbaits should be fished. If you are not fishing in the thick stuff, you are not going to catch many bass.

bigger spinnerbait with larger blades. On other waters that are full of small bass, I might even use the bigger bait."

"There are millions of undersized bass in some waters," explains Clunn, "and I would probably go to a little larger spinnerbait so that it would discourage some of the little fish. Culling by increasing the size of the lure should be an option."

Shaft And Blade Selections

Thin spinnerbait shafts are in vogue currently. Many feel that they are responsible for more strikes. The main problem with them, however, is that they are not as durable as some using larger diameter wire. They are prone to being torn up easier by an average-size bass.

A spinnerbait that has caught 10 or 15 fish has done more than most lures ever will. Thin-shaft spinnerbaits are prone to breakage after that number of fish, so knowledgeable anglers don't take a chance on it. They use a new one.

Big blades cause more wear on thin shafts than do the smaller blades. The wire on the some spinnerbaits is tapered down to the blades, and that makes them a little more durable than ones using the constant-diameter thin wire.

Obviously, a blade running on a thinner wire shaft will have more freedom than those off a thicker-shafted bait. More vibrations are possible at slow speeds with large blades on thinner shafts, and even at faster speeds, they perform well. Clunn prefers a tandem-bladed lure constructed with a small silver blade in front and a small willow leaf on the back.

Skirt Selections

The spinnerbait is a great tool, and with the transparent skirt it has more flexibility than it has ever had. The skirts, originally designed for jigs, allow a wide variety of metal flake colors to be used. Clunn normally fishes white and chartreuse spinnerbaits. The new plastics can be matched to the leadhead or the hues may be different.

"The skirt is very functional and actually allows you to fish a lot clearer water than most people would fish with a spinnerbait in the past," notes Clunn. "I had some doubts about it lasting long when I first saw the plastic vinyl skirt. I thought the bass would make the bottom ragged. It's very durable, however."

Clunn was impressed with the new skirts the first time he laid eyes on them. He was on the way to a national tournament and was able to get only two colors: motor oil and clear with silver flake. The pro felt that they would imitate the threadfin shad perfectly.

"Stripers work the open water and with the wind, combine to herd the shad into the windward coves," he explains. "Bass just lay in the windy coves and wait on the shad."

In the high winds, Clunn made long casts and ripped the lure back to the boat, without letting the two blades break the surface of the water. He could get away with using 15-pound test in the clear waters, since there was very little line touching the water.

"I was impressed with how deep they were sucking in the bait," he says. "The strong winds, pushing waves over the boat's bow in some cases, were making things difficult, though. I was bulging the surface with the lure, except when the waves got too big, I had to drop the bait."

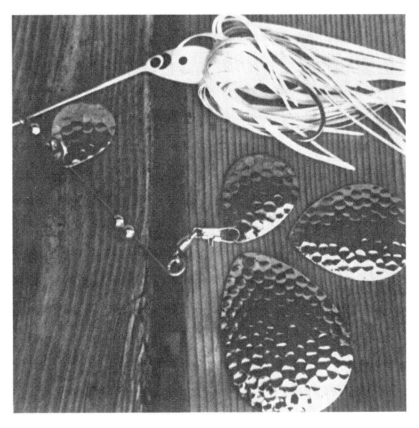

The flash and vibration pattern of a spinnerbait can be altered by changing the blade shape or size.

Trailer Thoughts

Trailer hooks are not given a lot of thought, until a big bass escapes a spinnerbait without one. They often pay for themselves with just one extra fish. That makes the addition of one worthwhile.

The conditions of the water and the habitat being fished should dictate whether or not a trailer hook is used. If it is costing you efficiency, it may be costing you in fish. By hanging up more often, the lure is not working toward the catch as often.

Use of plastic trailers behind the spinnerbait is common, as long as they don't interfere with the trailer hook. Clunn advises using either a split-tail eel or a small ring worm with a curl tail behind the spinnerbait. On big fish waters, however, he will opt for a little bigger gator tail worm trailer.

There are lots of things that can be done with a spinnerbait. The state of technological design will be advanced even more in the near future. In fact, I've designed one myself that should enhance productivity tremendously. It's not in production yet, but look out!

CHAPTER 10

SPOON SHAKIN'

An Effective Heavy-Cover Tactic

GREAT LURE TECHNIQUES seldom escape secrecy, but when one does, word quickly gets out. A new, unique near-surface concept involves a long rod, fairly heavy line, a 1/2 ounce spoon with plastic grub trailer and heavy cover.

When bass are buried in dense vegetation, they are often difficult to entice from their lair. While flippin' is one technique that is very effective on concentrated fish, it is usually too slow for locating them. If an angler is relatively unfamiliar with a lake or stream or hasn't fished it lately, he'll be looking for fish first. The "shakin' spoon" method will enable him to find the bass and draw them out for capture.

This spoon technique is best suited for heavy cover, such as hydrilla, grass or heavy pad fields. The preferred equipment by some experienced anglers is a 6 1/2 foot rod, 17 to 20-pound test Trilene XT line and a half-ounce black Johnson spoon with a yellow two-inch flat tail grub.

Most anglers don't use a trailer hook on the spoon. In fact, they don't alter it at all. The only thing necessary is to make sure that the hook is extremely sharp.

The spoon is a powerful weapon on shallow lakes with heavy vegetation. The spoon is tied directly to the line without a swivel, and the grub with the flat-type tail makes it much easier to work. It will quickly come to the top and will more easily stay on top with the trailer additive.

The grub has an action itself and doesn't deter the action of the spoon. According to some anglers, that's the key!

Larry Lazoen, a South Florida guide, has perfected the technique over the past few years to amass huge tallies of heavyweight bass. Most largemouth have been released, as Lazoen is very

This spoon technique is best suited for heavy cover, such as cypress swamps, grass or heavy pad fields.

conservation-minded, but the continual action for his clients and friends who duplicate the method is what has resulted in its newly established popularity.

Hard Strikes

Lazoen's best stringer in a day's time using the technique was 20 bass, which would have weighed around 50 pounds. All were released. Seldom does he, or anyone for that matter, miss many fish with this technique because bass hit it so aggressively.

"It's almost like crankbait fishing," he says. "When they hit it, they really hit it! If you simply pause one second, drop your rod tip down and snatch it up; he'll be on there."

"You make a cast and retrieve it almost as fast as you would a buzzbait," says Lazoen. "You need to keep the spoon moving very quickly, and as you reel it across the cover, you gently shake your wrist," he advises. "That makes the spoon slap both the water and the cover."

The lure moves quickly across the cover giving off a slapping sound. This results, more often than not, in a reaction strike. When the bass are tight to dense cover, they are usually not ruled by hunger. Surprisingly, it doesn't take much open water for a fish to come up and catch the disturbing source.

It's not a hard technique to master, but it is one that requires some practice to make it a real effective method. A 1/4 ounce spoon or a 3/4 ounce spoon, can be used, but the 1/2 ounce lure is often a favorite of knowledgeable fishermen.

Anglers can fish fast with this technique and cover a lot of water. Often, several casts to different pads won't result in a strike. But when the spoon goes by a pad that's home to a bass, that fish will hit it!

Heavy Cover Placement

"The spoon should be kept right on top," says Lazoen. "It should be shakin' and hoppin' and just making a lot of commotion on top. To do that, though, you don't want to overexaggerate the wrist-shaking," he advises.

"Very seldom will you get hangups if the spoon is fished correctly," says Lazoen. "With a long rod, the angle between the line and the water's surface is greater, and that has a tendency to keep the nose of the spoon higher, which minimizes hangups. It's an excellent way to fish pads. If you try to run the spoon under the water in scattered pads, it'll hang up on you."

Shakin' the spoon is an excellent technique in any kind of cover. It will work 11 months a year, on bedding fish, on pre- and post-spawn fish or even in the heat of summer. Lazoen feels that it is an excellent technique for big bass in the heat of the day, because they like to get up under the pads in some of the shallower water. With this technique, the lunkers are accessible.

Nutrient-rich lakes are ideal for this technique because there is so much heavy cover in the form of aquatic vegetation. The pH levels in the area of plantlife is usually more conducive to attracting and holding bass and their forage. It is usually notably higher around the vegetation than over barren water.

Bass in such dense surroundings may be aggressive fish and respond well to this technique. Many lakes throughout the country have the water chemistry and kind of cover in which to work this lure. If the fish are there, the lure and technique will find them.

PRIME SPOTS FOR SPOON SHAKIN'

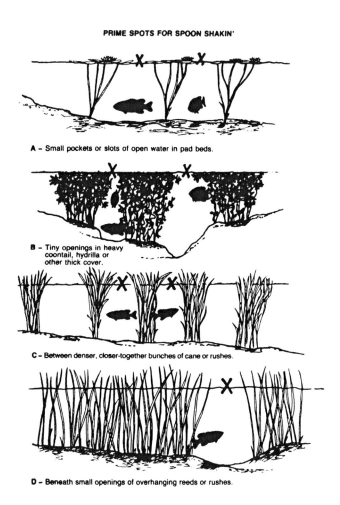

A - Small pockets or slots of open water in pad beds.

B - Tiny openings in heavy coontail, hydrilla or other thick cover.

C - Between denser, closer-together bunches of cane or rushes.

D - Beneath small openings of overhanging reeds or rushes.

FIGURE 9—*In most shallower fertile waters, profuse vegetation serves as home for numerous bass during the warmer months. Often, this vegetation encompasses more volume at the surface and leaves less dense cover nearer the bottom. Shaking a spoon in the small holes of open surface water within the vegetation should result in some explosions.*

The Port Charlotte fisherman has used it successfully in many lakes throughout the South. When not on the water as a full time guide, Lazoen teaches fresh and salt water fishing classes. The effectiveness and correct retrieve procedure for the spoon is an integral part of his classes when instructing largemouth bass techniques.

Standard vs. Shakin'

"This technique seems to work better than most of the standard ways of working the spoon," says Lazoen. "I've fished on lakes where buddies in other boats were using the same combination but retrieving more in a traditional manner. They were slowly working it with a steady, wobbling retrieve and letting it fall into holes or were running the spoon a little deeper, just under the surface."

"At the end of the day, we would compare our catches and what we were doing. I was surprised to find out that some days, when I had done so well fishing the same kind of cover, they had very small catches. These were explosive fish that were very aggressive and very active!"

On the following day, Lazoen's friends went out and applied the shakin' technique and found out that the fish were actually there. Those bass just wanted a faster, noisier bait. The technique produced much better for them after that also.

This technique prior to the spawn has produced some outstanding stringers of five and six-pound largemouth, and sometimes there are seven and eight-pounders right in there with them. Near a major spawning area there is usually a staging area, where the bigger fish will congregate prior to moving into the spawning grounds. If you're familiar with such an area or find one similar, this spoon method will really help find more and larger fish.

Pre-Spawn Staging Areas

"That happened to me one spring on Lake Okeechobee," says Lazoen. "There is a major spawning ground there, and the two pools

Shallow, two-foot deep pools are typical staging areas that bass use before they move on further into the area to spawn. Quality fish will move into such pools and hold there until moving in to spawn.

had dollar pads covering two feet of water. It was deeper there than on the spawning grounds, and the bass staged up there."

That area has only a narrow boat-width trail going in and out, running three or four city blocks long through a wall of cattails. Then, it breaks open into a depression that is about one foot deeper than the actual spawning grounds. Another trail leaves that one and goes into a smaller pool.

The spawning grounds are probably 3/4 mile from the first pool and 1/4 mile from the second one. These are typical of the staging areas that bass use before they move on further into the area to spawn. Quality fish will move into such pools and hold there until moving in to spawn. The shakin' spoon will allow you to catch some healthy pre-spawners.

While Lazoen doesn't recommend fishing for spawning bass, they can be caught on the shakin' spoon. An angler must drop down to 14 pound test and use the long rod to make very long casts with the 1/2 ounce spoon. When the lure is popped across the beds, the bass just can't resist it. They'll get up and get it!

There are many areas throughout the country that offer shallow water bedding areas. The technique is productive, even if the bass are not spawning, because these fish will move into the heavy cover in these same areas when it gets hot. Post- spawners seem to move into nearby pads or other cover to recuperate. They're in a feeding mood, though, which is an excellent situation for the shakin' spoon.

During the spring, summer or fall, this technique will add weight to the stringer. Just find a highly vegetated body of water, add a spoon and grub combination, then shake well for the bass action of your life.

CHAPTER 11

TOP WATER TRICKS

Crazy Techniques And Plug Creations

THEY COULD BE PLAYFUL, hungry or mad, or even a combination of the three. Largemouth bass that strike a surface plug are hard to figure out.

What motivates them to slam a bait on the fringe of their environment is difficult to establish. Certainly, the action and looks of an artificial may command the response of the bass. Often he'll miss his target and come back. At other times, the fish will soon be long gone.

Lure designers have spent hours trying to perfect the top water plug that will always attract and hook bass. Some attempts have been partially successful; others have not come close. Technique variations often are responsible for increased attraction and resulting strikes.

I can remember carving two or three versions of my own surface plug some 15 years ago. One in particular was unique; the lure had a worm trailer that was free to dance behind the plug. I caught fish with the bait, but it was not super productive.

Regardless of the rather inconsistent production, bass anglers everywhere have developed a love for top water plugs. Many also have worked overtime to develop effective techniques for the lures. Others have modified plugs to fool more bass.

Such baits are responsible for fish in all parts of the country. Usually, word of productive modifications are slow to 'leak out.' Successful rigs tend to be local secrets; that is, until bass professionals learn about them and rely on them in other parts of the bass world.

The Boat People

"Top water fishing is the most exciting way to fish," points out bass guide, Randy Dearman. "A unique plug that's successful on Sam Rayburn Lake is called a 'boat'."

The odd-looking lure is carved from a piece of balsa wood to a length of about 3 inches. The floating plug is an inch wide and packs a single 4/0 stainless steel hook that sticks straight up out of it. The lure will float on top of extremely heavy vegetation, regardless of how matted it may be.

Dearman suggests that the lure is easy to make, and with the results it has generated, its success record is significant. Many East Texas anglers and guides have carved their own versions, and most seem to catch bass under the right conditions.

The balsa wood shape should be similar to a spoon and flat on the bottom so it won't roll over, according to Dearman. The "boat" then will come right across the top of the thickest weeds. It should not get hung.

"I like to fish a bait like this in heavy grass and vary the retrieve," says the Texan. "Sometimes, the largemouth want the bait that's fished slow, and at other times, they'll hit a fast-retrieved lure."

He prefers to cast the "boat" to the edges of all pockets or holes in the thick grass. In fact, Dearman advises against pulling it across the middle of a hole.

"You don't have to penetrate the grass," explains Dearman. "This top water bait will draw them to the surface. If you keep it on the edges, you'll catch more fish," he says.

Surface Customizing

Other customizing tricks are used by professional bassmen and plain ol' weekend anglers. Try some of the following when the action slows on top. Naturally, most modifications and experimentation should be done prior to visiting the lake.

• File down the lower lip of a chugger lure so that it won't gulp so

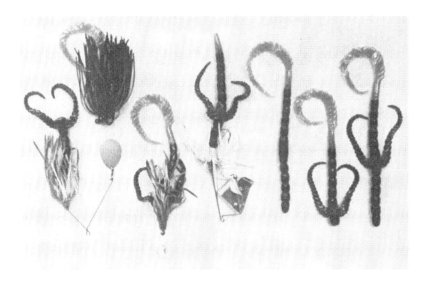

Fooling a big bass on surface baits is sometimes difficult, but special modifications can be made, even to bottom bumping plastics, that will boost your success rate.

much water as it's twitched. Less disturbance in calm waters is often more productive.

• Twist the propeller blades of a prop bait in opposite directions to make them turn easier. The easier the blades spin, the more productive they are at times.

• Snip off the front hook on each treble to make the plug more weedless. Fish it in heavier cover with added assurance of few hangups.

• Use a heavy line, e.g. 20 pound test, to keep the floating bait on the surface. Large diameter line is more buoyant and allows the plug to be worked on top as it's often intended to be.

Such a list could probably continue for pages. Most anglers have ideas about modifications. Cutting lips off buoyant diving plugs works at times, but possibly the technique or retrieve is responsible for bass strikes. After all, a lure without action must smell and taste awful good for any fish to be interested in chewing on such.

Technique is also a significant variable. Some anglers have developed their own way of enticing largemouth strikes. Very successful anglers often resort to special methods in order to fool the bass.

Vicious Strike Strategy

Tommy Martin utilizes a specific 'trick' when fishing surface plugs in the late summer and early fall. Largemouth bass will often come up and 'boil' a topwater lure and he has relied on a technique that will often put that fish in the boat.

"Sometimes, they'll even strike viciously at it and jump completely over the topwater plug," he says. "That activity gives away the location of the fish, though, and these fish can be caught," adds Martin.

Once a bass strikes at a topwater lure and misses its mark, anglers should let that surface plug sit and use a sinking or descending bait instead. A crankbait, such as a Rat-L-Trap, or a worm cast back on top of the fish should be successful.

"There is something about a topwater plug that will sometimes get the fish to come up and boil at it, but not take it," says Martin. "You have to immediately throw back on these fish before they have time to leave the area. They'll still be near that topwater plug, trying to decide whether or not to strike at it again."

Most anglers find that this tactic works on largemouth that miss the plug's hooks most of the time. In fact, the technique would be effective any time a lot of short strikes happen with any type of topwater plug. While this technique is pretty well known, few anglers are very proficient at it.

Sitting Still

Normally, the most effective way to use a top water lure is to let it sit until the ripples completely die and then move it slowly. The longer it's around fish, the more time he has to look at it and the more bass you're going to catch. Productive anglers will usually vary the retrieve until they find an aggressive fish that will hit it.

Bigger bass, it seems, will usually hit the prop-type bait quicker when you pull it just under the surface than if you leave it on top. They won't explode on it like they might with other types of topwater lures being pulled faster, though. They'll just come up and suck it under.

The smaller-type baits are more productive on schoolers in the summer, and the jumper-type baits seem to be more effective in the early fall. Making a lot of commotion on the surface with the plugs will produce more fish consistently, but in early spring and later in the fall, the less you move the bait, the better off you may be. It takes a lot of patience to fish that way, but it can pay off.

Many productive techniques are obvious, once the reasoning is explained. For example, an erratic plug like the Zara Spook is usually more productive when used in clear waters. Why would this be the case when a Spook is being "walked" back to the boat? Bass need to be able to see the change in movement to successfully strike it. That's why.

The author enjoys a good tussle on top, but often it takes more time enticing the strike than landing the lunker bass.

Surface Tricks

An erratically-retrieved plug in muddy waters may generate several swirls and misses, but the bass will seldom connect. Save the erratic retrieves for the waters that are at least semi-clear.

Some other tricks to try are:

• Instead of leaving a plug sit after a missed strike, quickly reel in an "escape" mode. That is what happens in the underwater environment when a small panfish has a near catastrophic encounter with a bigmouth.

• Try reeling the surface plug underneath the water to produce a strike. The action may be enticing to draw an impulse strike from a bass.

• Wait out a bass that has missed the plug. The chances are good that the fish is still observing its "prey." Let it sit for three or four minutes before twiching it.

Drawing surface strikes from our quarry often takes patience and persistence, but it is an exciting form of aquatic enjoyment. Varying the standard techniques to entice a top water encounter is often required for a reward.

Whether you add weight to the hooks of your topwater plugs, add larger hooks to it or modify it in another way, you'll take some pride in catching bass on the "new version." In fact, fooling a bass on top with lures out of the box and a 'standard' retrieve is something to be proud of.

CHAPTER 12

DIFFERENT RIGGINGS

Unique Modifications And Methods

WHEN THE FISHING'S tough, the tough usually get going. Plugs right out of the box don't always slay bass, and the Texas-rigged worm doesn't always catch the most bass. What do the experienced anglers come up with to put together a productive pattern when the bass have supposedly stopped biting?

There are little tricks that successful fishermen employ to give them an edge over inactive bass. Often, it's a slightly different technique; sometimes it's a lure modification that makes a difference. Once you've been around bunches of anglers for a few years, you will quickly learn that changes and alterations to lures and methods are commonplace. Many don't work, but some do.

One method used frequently in crankbait and spinnerbait fishing, especially when the fish are not aggressive at all, is to move the rod tip to attain extra sensitivity. Crank with the rod tip down as usual, but move it to one side or the other at about a 20 to 30 degree angle.

The movement allows the rod tip to be loaded a bit more than usual, increasing an angler's sensitivity. It will be easier then to feel those slight nudges or bumps that might otherwise not be detected.

When approaching a key target, stop reeling and move the lure past the object with the rod tip.

"The less motion you have—your hands and arms working against each other—the more you're going to feel," says Batesville, Mississippi pro, Harold Allen. "This tactic is especially productive on light-hitting, inactive fish."

In worm fishing, contrary to most anglers, Allen prefers to feel resistance on the line rather than a tap tap. "I like to work my worm on the bottom with the rod tip high (10 to 12 o'clock) with some slack line," the pro explains.

Not all plugs right out of the box catch fish every time. Modifications may increase their effectiveness.

"If your line is tight while working the worm, the fish will feel you as soon as you feel him. If the fish isn't really active, or he's in a finicky mood, this resistance could be enough for him to drop the lure," says Allen. "With the slack line approach, the fish hits the lure, feels no resistance and will hold the lure longer, allowing the angler more time to set up."

Trim Tactic

Regardless of the methods employed, subtle changes to a bait may increase its effectiveness in certain situations and/or conditions. Lots of anglers change or modify their baits, and the jig and plastic combinations are among those with which anglers experiment.

Jigs occupy a prime place in most anglers' arsenal. For years, Allen has fished Arkie jigs in bodies of water all over the country.

He first started fishing a living rubber jig during the summer, and he chose a Norman Snatrix for the trailer.

"Plastic trailers seem to be better than pork in the hot time of the year," he claims. "Fish are more active and chase a bait more readily then. The Snatrix has both the appearance of a bulky, big fish bait and a swimming-tail action."

It worked well enough as a trailer for Allen to win a couple of tournaments on it, but he did make a slight alteration to the bait. The lure has a head, small neck and then about an inch and one-half of body (excluding the tail). He would cut the head of the Snatrix off, which would allow the body to slide up on the shank of the jig hook.

"It really stayed on the hook then," he says. "I would catch five or six bass and it would still be on there."

Allen prefers the Snatrix over a regular grub tail because of the maximum swimming action exhibited beyond the end of the rubber skirt. On many of the jigs, unless you trim the rubber skirts, two-thirds of the plastic trailer is covered. The bait has enough length to get out past the rubber and produce good swimming action, according to Allen.

A second factor probably contributes to its success as a trailer—the thin ribbon tail. After the jig has plunged to the bottom and stopped, the plastic trailer tries to retain its original shape (curled). The thin plastic curls back up and "breathes" too.

Unique riggings are used regionally and the word seldom spreads far. Others are so successful and highly promoted through the outdoor media that the world seems to know of the new technique or bait modification. A regional offering that is very productive is a plastic worm technique that guides use on Toledo Bend. It is different.

Whacki Worm

"In all my fishing travels, I have never seen this technique used," says Tommy Martin. "We call it a whacki worm and it has been used on Toledo Bend for several years."

Seasonal Lure Size Variation

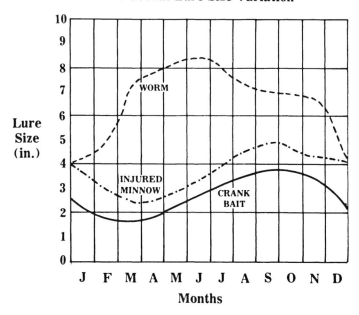

FIGURE 10—*Lure size selection should vary during the year for maximum productivity. As spring wanes and young of the year forage begins to grow, so should the size of the bait.*

"We take a 6-inch worm and insert a roofing nail with the head cut off into the head of the worm," he explains. "The roofing nail does two things: it provides additional weight so we can cast the worm better, and it gives the worm action once it gets into the water."

Martin claims that they have tried other worms but the 6-inch Creme Scoundrel works the best. He feels that's because it is molded with a harder plastic than most worms and it has the straight do-nothing tail that works best for this presentation. You need a hard plastic worm so you can insert a 1/0 worm hook through its midsection and make repeated casts without tearing up the worm.

This technique works best during the spring, when the bass are in extremely shallow water or on spawning beds. On Toledo Bend, Martin reports that they fish the whacki worm behind the hydrilla grass lines, between the grass line and the bank, or in any opening you can see in the grass. Hangups with the exposed hook is not really the problem one might expect.

"We fish the whacki worm with a medium light action rod with casting or open-faced spinning reel and 10 pound Trilene XT line," explains Martin. "The worm is real easy to fish. Simply cast it out and either reel the worm back very slowly just under the water or pump the worm with your rod, let it fall towards the bottom and then reel up the slack and pump it again."

"You will actually see most of the bass you can catch on the whacki worm come up and inhale it," Martin points out. "Fishing it is somewhat like fishing a topwater, imitation-minnow plug. You must let the bass run about a foot with the worm for best hooking results," he cautions.

The technique is deadly on the East Texas lake during the spring, particularly on a bright, clear day with no wind. That's when those

A six-inch, hard plastic worm with a roofing nail inserted into the head and a 1/0 worm hook through the belly is sometimes called the "Whacki Worm."

shallow water bass just don't seem to want to strike anything else. The conditions are similar in other parts of the country at times, and the bass probably haven't seen this productive ploy.

Spook Buster

A new 'twist' in lure modifications surfaced a few years ago on Missouri's Table Rock Lake. The lure, a modified Zara Spook, was utilized by several professionals and proved to be very effective at enticing large bass.

The lure, whether modified or not, resembles an injured thread-fin or gizzard shad when twitched on the surface. Anglers who 'walk the dog' with it, causing the lure to alternately nose forward in one direction and then another, often attract bass from several feet away in the clear water.

Some western-based bass pros came up with the idea by doing some homework, literally. They went to the workbench and made some changes to Heddon's successful topwater plug. They first took off the tie eye and rear treble hook and used epoxy to seal the resulting holes in the bait. The treble hook attached to the belly was left alone.

Two small holes were then drilled into the plastic plug body one-quarter inch away from the plugged ones. A piece of surgical tubing was then threaded in one hole and out the other. The tubing lying along the inside of the plug was epoxied in place on the exterior and any excess snipped off. This tube thus provided a 'line guide' through the Spook's body.

On the water, 14 pound-test monofilament was then threaded through the tube and out the tail end, through a one-quarter inch diameter red bead, through a shad-colored Gits-It, and then through a 1/8 oz. slip sinker (tail to nose in this application). The plastic Gits-It is a recent grub bait development that resembles a hollow squid in appearance.

The slip sinker actually snugs up tightly inside the hollow grub and provides weight for that portion of the rig. A #4 treble hook at the terminal end of the line completes the rig, and, when snugged up

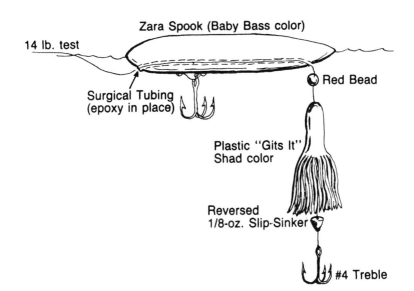

Zara Spook (Baby Bass color)

14 lb. test

Surgical Tubing
(epoxy in place)

Red Bead

Plastic "Gits It"
Shad color

Reversed
1/8-oz. Slip-Sinker

#4 Treble

FIGURE 11—*The modified Zara Spook catches fish but also draws a lot of swirls from near misses. When that occurs, slack line is given so the grub falls back down to the fish. When line is drawn tight, sinker and treble hook shank are hidden inside hollow grub body. The front eye-tie and rear treble screw are taken out, and their holes are epoxied water tight.*

to the lure inside the Gits-It body, only the points are exposed through the plastic 'tentacles'.

The Spook attracts attention, and swirls are often misses. With the modified rig, however, those boils are often caught. When a miss occurs, slack line is given to the rig and the weighted Gits-It and tail-affixed treble hook descend toward the bottom. The bass that was reluctant to hit the surface bait is usually much more eager to suck in the falling Gits-It. Today, there's a production model of that bait on the market.

Other modifications to lures may last as secrets longer. In reaction-type baits, some anglers want the hooks to have a wider bite. They'll bend the points out slightly, though, rather than go with larger hooks. Others will add split rings to baits that don't have them to allow the hooks to swing easier. Still others might add lead solder to the hook shanks of some topwater baits, which tends to make them suspend, rather than float.

The modified rigs described here are ones that will allow some anglers to catch more bass when they experience unusual situations on the lake. When the bass aren't hitting, try a unique lure or tactic.

CHAPTER 13

LURE COLOR SELECTIONS

State-Of-The-Art Means

MOST BASS RELY greatly on their color vision while foraging. Knowing how water and light characteristics affect their selection process will enable an angler to choose more effective lure colors and entice the aggressive feeders.

While theories have been expressed over the years, until recently very little has been proven about color selection preferences of bass. Most anglers' "best guess" was based on individual experiences over the years. What we selected from the tackle box was the lure that seemed to have worked on a similar day. We based the bait color choice on such 'factors' as cloud cover, water clarity, angle of the sun and water depth.

Often, the chosen 'weapon' worked, and numerous bass were caught on a specific lure. But just as often, "educated guesses" were wrong, and largemouth were not to be found.

A couple of years ago, research information became available that confirmed many anglers' field observations. The findings by Dr. Loren Hill, the University of Oklahoma professor who developed the pH monitor, also refute certain long-established 'theories' regarding color preference of bass.

Dr. Hill's nine years of research on the color sensitivity of largemouth and their reactions to color presentation at given water visibilities and light penetrations should be of interest to all anglers. The chairman of the University's Zoology Department, and Director of Biological Research, has formulated several conclusions based on careful behavioral observations.

Testing of bass feeding action and reaction produced results which correspond to lure color preference. Field tests by Dr. Hill, professional anglers Bill Dance, Ken Cook, Al Lindner, Jimmy Houston, and many others have proven the value of the laboratory work. The study behind the creation of the Color-C-Lector certainly provides food for thought.

Fish Eye View

The fish's eye functions to receive, resolve and respond to light and detect movement, form and color. Research has proven that! In fact, tests have shown bass have excellent color vision and can distinguish between narrow color bands. They can even discriminate between different shades of the same color. In most situations and conditions, their sighting abilities are the dominant sense used for seeking and selecting food.

The photo sensory cells in a fish's retina are made up of cones (for color vision) and rods (for black and white vision). Because of their anatomy, a fish's eye can receive five times more light than the human eye, allowing them to distinguish shapes, sizes, and color patterns the human eye can't, and fish can do this under varying water and light conditions!

Their eyes also contain a black pigment (not present in human eyes) that shades the photo-sensitive cells of the retina and allows them to see equally well in extremely bright conditions with no discomfort. Without eyelids, they need that feature.

Dr. Hill's color research began by establishing a full range of 26 colors that fish could distinguish best. The test subjects were collected from a variety of habitats in central and southern Oklahoma, i.e., Lake Texoma, Lake Carter, and several farm ponds. The largemouth bass were introduced into circular 5,000 gallon holding tanks at the University's Biological Station laboratory and were maintained for one week in the aerated, filtered and temperature-controlled (72 degrees) environment prior to experimentation.

The fish were each tested individually in experimental chambers that differed from the holding facility. Dr. Hill first trained the bass to strike a circular target that was suspended into one of the chambers. In another, he placed a series of colored plates symmetrically around the periphery and used a copper grid on the bottom to provide a mild shock for training purposes. In the third experimental

Dr. Loren Hill spent nine years doing research on the bass color selectivity, so that anglers can base their lure choices on scientific fact.

chamber, a release-trough allowed eleven objects to be released simultaneously.

Testing Results

Results showed the bass to be sensitive to all colors tested, and that they could discriminate between colors green, blue green, light green, and dark green. The bass were even able to determine different shades of the same color. The collective data suggested that bass have a preference for the color green and may be adverse to the color yellow. Red was determined to be somewhat intermediate in color preference during the testing.

Fluorescent color preference tests resulted in data suggesting blue and green to be favorites. While fluorescent red and orange were intermediate in reference to the response of the bass, the most negative reactions recorded were for fluorescent colors combined with yellow. In further experimentation, the light factor and the water clarity were manipulated to simulate environmental conditions.

"To simulate different fishing conditions, visibility was varied from clear (4 ft. and greater) to stained (2 to 4 feet) to muddy (2 feet or less)" says Dr. Hill. "Sky conditions, overcast or clear, were simulated for early morning (5 to 6 a.m.), mid-morning (9:30 a.m. to 10:30 a.m.), noon, (to 1 p.m.) mid-afternoon (3:30 p.m. to 4:30 p.m.) and night (7:30 p.m. to 8:30 p.m.) periods."

Numerous graphs and charts were generated from the carefully measured testing, and the data suggests that bass can see blue, yel-

The Multi-C-Lector, a product of years of on-the-water testing, reveals water chemistry characteristics, as well as the optimal lure color.

low, white, silver and purple best under these environmental conditions and that black, grey, and red are not highly visible to the fish. Fluorescent tests revealed that a significant shift in color sensitivity occurred as conditions varied in clear water. While these differences were obvious, results showed the most sensitive colors are not consistent from one water clarity to another under other similar conditions.

Environmental Variables

Of the environmental conditions manipulated in these experiments, the most significant effects upon the ability of the bass to see color were the water clarity, i.e., clear, stained, or muddy, and the hour of the day. The least influential factor on the ability of the bass to determine shades of color was whether the sky was clear or overcast.

From Dr. Hill's data, it was deducted that the bass can detect a wide variety of non fluorescent and fluorescent colors under various environmental conditions. However, the degree of sensitivity of the bass to fluorescent colors was, for the most part, consistently stronger than their responses to non- fluorescent colors, under most conditions.

The colored food preferences were found to be strongly influenced by water clarity and time of day. The degree of correlation between the color sensitivity experiments and color of food item eaten under similar environmental conditions was extremely high.

During the experiments, the exact light transmittance value was recorded by means of a light meter, reading 0 to 100 percent. Subsequently, the color preference data was transformed onto the dial of a light meter, measuring percentage of light transmitted. The color spectrum reflected the results of Dr. Hill's extensive tests. The Color-C-Lector was born.

"By dropping the light meter probe into the water at any depth, a percentage value of light transmittancy will appear." says Dr. Hill. "That is then correlated to the color most visible to the bass under the particular water clarity, time of day, and sky condition."

From the color selectivity tests, several generalities can be made regarding lure color choices under given conditions. The author often verifies his experienced-based selections with the instrument.

"Not only does the instrument point to the color most visible and color of food item or lure preferred, but one can determine the best combination of colors," he adds. "For example, the colors adjacent to the color pointed to on the band would be the right combo. The instrument will predict with extreme reliability the lure color combination which will receive from 90 to 100 percent of the strikes!"

The Best Colors

Several generalities are evident from Dr. Hill's tests. A color preference that many know, for example, is "black" in clear water at night, with or without moon. Anglers knowing this have succeeded at fooling a lunker bass with a black spinnerbait or topwater plug at night from a local, gin-clear lake.

From his color chart, other generalities can be made. The color "grey" is generally a good selection between 10 a.m. and 2 p.m., regardless of water clarity. "Silver" lures should be productive when the sun is at a lower angle, say during the time periods 8:30 a.m. to 10:30 a.m. and 1:30 p.m. to 3:30 p.m.

The sun angle between 8:30 a.m. and 3:30 p.m. just happens to coincide with the major active period of threadfin shad, a favorite forage of the largemouth. Gray and silver colors are close to the actual hue of the baitfish.

The Color-C-Lector and following generation, Multi-C-Lector, (which additionally identifies a multitude of water chemistry characteristics) seem to be a good way of getting some intelligent assistance in choosing the best color of lure to toss.

BASS SERIES LIBRARY!

Eight Great Books With A Wealth Of Information
For Bass Fishermen
By Larry Larsen

I. FOLLOW THE FORAGE FOR BETTER BASS ANGLING - VOLUME 1 BASS/ PREY RELATIONSHIP - The most important key to catching bass is finding them in a feeding mood. Knowing the predominant forage, its activity and availability, as well as its location in a body of water will enable an angler to catch more and larger bass. Whether you fish artificial lures or live bait, you will benefit from this book.

SPECIAL FEATURES   o PREDATOR/FORAGE INTERACTION
                            o BASS FEEDING BEHAVIOR
                            o UNDERSTANDING BASS FORAGE
                            o BASS/PREY PREFERENCES
                            o FORAGE ACTIVITY CHART

II. FOLLOW THE FORAGE FOR BETTER BASS ANGLING - VOLUME 2 TECH-NIQUES - Beginners and veterans alike will achieve more success utilizing proven concepts that are based on predator/forage interactions. Understanding the reasons behind lure or bait success will result in highly productive, bass-catching patterns.

SPECIAL FEATURES   o LURE SELECTION CRITERIA
                            o EFFECTIVE PATTERN DEVELOPMENT
                            o NEW BASS CATCHING TACTICS
                            o FORAGING HABITAT
                            o BAIT AND LURE METHODS

III. BASS PRO STRATEGIES - Professional fishermen have opportunities to devote extended amounts of time to analyzing a body of water and planning a productive day on it. They know how changes in pH, water temperature, color and fluctuations affect bass fishing, and they know how to adapt to weather and topographical variations. This book reveals the methods that the country's most successful tournament anglers have employed to catch bass almost every time out. The reader's productivity should improve after spending a few hours with this compilation of techniques!

SPECIAL FEATURES   o MAPPING & WATER ELIMINATION
   o LOCATE DEEP & SHALLOW BASS
   o BOAT POSITION FACTORS
   o WATER CHEMISTRY INFLUENCES
   o WEATHER EFFECTS
   o TOPOGRAPHICAL TECHNIQUES

IV. BASS LURES - TRICKS & TECHNIQUES - Modifications of lures and development of new baits and techniques continue to keep the fare fresh, and that's important. Bass seem to become "accustomed" to the same artificials and presentations seen over and over again. As a result, they become harder to catch. It's the new approach that again sparks the interest of some largemouth. To that end, this book explores some of the latest ideas for modifying, rigging and using them. The lure modifications, tricks and techniques presented within these covers will work anywhere in the country.

SPECIAL FEATURES   o UNIQUE LURE MODIFICATIONS
   o IN-DEPTH VARIABLE REASONING
   o PRODUCTIVE PRESENTATIONS
   o EFFECTIVE NEW RIGGINGS
   o TECHNOLOGICAL ADVANCES

V. SHALLOW WATER BASS - Catching shallow water largemouth is not particularly difficult. Catching lots of them usually is. Even more challenging is catching lunker-size bass in seasons other than during the spring spawn. Anglers applying the information within the covers of this book on marshes, estuaries, reservoirs, lakes, creeks or small ponds should triple their results. The book details productive new tactics to apply to thin-water angling. Numerous photographs and figures easily define the optimal locations and proven methods to catch bass.

SPECIAL FEATURES   o UNDERSTANDING BASS/COVER INTERFACE
   o METHODS TO LOCATE BASS CONCENTRATIONS
   o ANALYSIS OF WATER TYPES
   o TACTICS FOR SPECIFIC HABITATS
   o LARSEN'S "FLORA FACTOR"

VI. BASS FISHING FACTS - This angler's guide to the lifestyles and behavior of the black bass is a reference source of sorts, never before compiled. The book explores the behavior of bass during pre- and post-spawn as well as during bedding season. It examines how bass utilize their senses to feed and how they respond to environmental factors. The book details how fishermen can be more productive by applying such knowledge to their bass angling. The information within the covers of this book includes those bass species, known as "other" bass, such as redeye, Suwannee, spotted, etc.

SPECIAL FEATURES   o BASS FORAGING MOTIVATORS
   o DETAILED SPRING MOVEMENTS
   o A LOOK AT BASS SENSES
   o GENETIC INTRODUCTION/STUDIES
   o MINOR BASS SPECIES & HABITATS

VII. TROPHY BASS - is focused at today's dedicated lunker hunters who find more enjoyment in wrestling with one or two monster largemouth than with a "panfull" of yearlings. To help the reader better understand how to catch big bass, a majority of this book explores productive techniques for trophies. The "how to" information was gleaned from professional guides and other experienced trophy bass hunters. This book takes a look at the geographical areas and waters that offer better opportunities to catch giant bass.

SPECIAL FEATURES   o GEOGRAPHIC DISTRIBUTIONS
        o STATE RECORD INFORMATION
        o GENETIC GIANTS
        o TECHNIQUES FOR TROPHIES
        o LOCATION CONSIDERATIONS
        o LURE AND BAIT TIMING

VIII. AN ANGLER'S GUIDE TO BASS PATTERNS examines the most effective combination of lure, method and places. Being able to develop a pattern of successful methods and lures for specific habitats and environmental conditions is the key to catching several bass on each fishing trip. Understanding bass movements and activities and the most appropriate and effective techniques to employ will add many pounds of enjoyment to the sport of bass fishing. "Bass Patterns" is a reference source for all anglers, regardless of where they live or their skill level.

SPECIAL FEATURES   o BOAT POSITIONING
        o NEW WATER STRATEGIES
        o DEPTH AND COVER CONCEPTS
        o MOVING WATER TACTICS
        o WEATHER/ACTIVITY FACTORS
        o TRANSITIONAL TECHNIQUES

WHAT OTHERS HAVE SAID ABOUT:

"BETTER BASS ANGLING"

".. . is sure to make a splash with the growing fraternity of bass anglers."
                                        —Colin Moore, Pensacola News Journal

".. . is a studious, meticulous approach to help you increase you success."
                                        —Michael Levy, Buffalo News

".. . gets to the meat of the matter."
                                        —Ben Callaway, Philadelphia Inquirer

".. . is a technical study of bass forage as the key to catching more largemouths."
                                        —Frank Sargeant, Tampa Tribune

".. . is the best how-to book to come off the press in years."
                                        —Johnny Pate, DeFuniak Springs Herald

".. . is 358 pages of bass lore gleaned from the nation's top scientists, recognized bass experts and lifetime of study on the part of Larsen."
                                        —Jerry Hill, Bradenton Herald

".. . will increase your knowledge, whether you are a serious tournament bass angler or a fun fisherman."
                                        —Del Milligan, Lakeland Ledger

".. . explores the forage-bass relationship in full."
                                        —Russell Tinsley, Austin Statesman

".. . is a book from which every serious bass angler can glean some food for thought to make him, or her, more successful on the water."
                                        —Tom Fegely, Allentown Call-Chronicle

".. . fills the void of books on bass behavior."
                                        —David Dunaway, Gainesville Sun

"... is one of the most informative books on bass fishing that I've read in the 80's."

—*Charles Salter, Atlanta Journal*

"... is loaded with information Larsen has accumulated in years of fishing for the wily bass."

—*Henry Reynolds, Memphis Commercial Appeal*

"... is a book every serious angler will want to own."

—*Charley Dickey, Tallahassee Democrat*

"... has the promise of becoming a classic on the bookshelves of serious bassers."

—*Russ Fee, Citrus County Chronicle*

"... goes right to the bass stomach to help you catch more fish."

—*St. Louis Outdoor News*

"... is one of the most complete books available on the subject."

—*Outdoor Life*

"... is a valuable book which I guarantee will help you understand what's going on down there where your lure is."

—*Jim Spencer, Pine Bluff Commercial*

"... is chock full of ideas and helpful hints to understanding the feeding habits and patterns of bass."

—*Glynn Harris, Shreveport Journal*

"SHALLOW WATER BASS"

"... helps the fisherman to develop a systematic approach to consistently locate bass."

—*Bill Sargent, Florida Today*

"... presents concepts which the bass angler should be able to apply to his home waters."

—*Byron Stout, Ft. Myers News Press*

". . . is the first book ever published that identifies particular methods that can be systematically applied to locate bass in shallow water."

—Bassin' magazine

". . . offers a lot for the novice, as well as for the tournament angler."

—Richard Bowles, Gainesville Sun

". . . offers tips and guides to increase both your strikes and actual landings of largemouth bass."

—Jerry Hill, Bradenton Herald

". . . is especially relevant for Florida fishermen who do most of their angling in water less than 10 feet deep."

—Frank Sargeant, Tampa Tribune